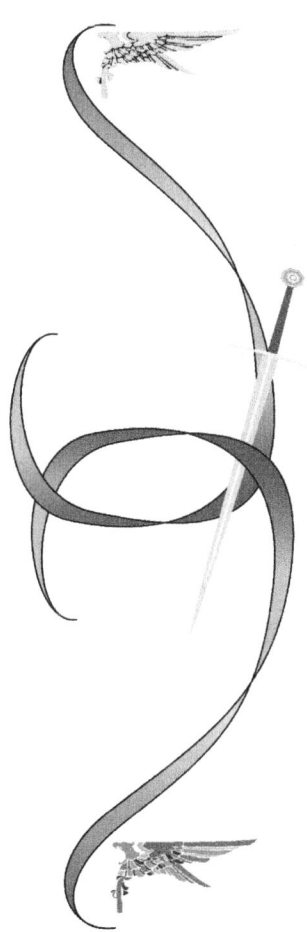

Faith on a Wing and a Prayer

© Copyright Sheri Hauser 2020
© Copyright Paul G. Hauser 2020 for Photo used on Cover
Published by Glorybound Publishing, Camp Verde
SAN 256-4564
3rd Edition
Printed in the United States of America
KDP ISBN   9798577562991
Copyright data is available on file.
Hauser, Sheri, 1957-
      Faith on a Wing and a Prayer/Sheri Hauser
      Includes biographical reference.
1. Religious/Prayer.   2. Charismatic interest/Dreams.   I. Title

www.gloryboundpublishing.com

The cover photo is taken by Paul G. Hauser flying at around 15,000 feet coming into Phoenix, Arizona during the summer monsoon season August 2012.

Dedicated to those who chose to live their lives on a wing and a prayer.

Sheri's Dream Books

And Afterwards I will Pour Out My Spirit
Christian Authors Driving the Market
Dream Language Understood
Faith on a Wing and a Prayer
Filled with the Holy Spirit
Foundational Prophetic Prayer
Going to the Center of God's Heart
Growing Ministry to Seed instead of Fruit
Inspirational 3-D Poetry
Intimate Relationship with Jesus
Leading Prophetic Prayer
Living in the Haunted House of my Head
Living in the Shadow of the Sins of our Parents
Personal Prophetic Prayer
Preparing the Bride of Christ: Allegorical
Prophetic Interpretation of Art
Sharing Prophetic Gifts in the Church
Simple Fun Christian Dream Interpretation
Spiritual Authority Over Demon Dragons
Tactical Demonic Warfare
Why the Glory Departed

Faith on a Wing and a Prayer

Kapaseus

By
Sheri Hauser

Glorybound Publishing
Camp Verde, Arizona
2020

Be Threaded

*We are like a needle in God's hand when grab hold of His dreams,
then run through the fabric of His intention.*

Letter from the Author

The capstone is used to seal the top of the stone fence. It is what brings together all of the other stones and tops the structure enabling it to become what is needed to do the job it was intended to do. The word also refers to the Mercy Seat which covered the Ark of the Covenant. It is what caps the plan that God has for meeting with us. In Exodus 25.21-22 it says; And thou shalt put the mercy seat above the ark; and in the ark thou shalt put the testimony that I shall give thee. And there I will meet with thee, and I will commune with thee from above the mercy seat, from between the two cherubims which are upon the ark of the testimony, of all things which I will give thee in commandment unto the children of Israel.

God met with them over the mercy seat between the two angels.
{Note that my logo has two angels, one on either side of the business name, because this is God's protection for me as I move forth within His purposes.} He is the one who provides us with mercy which enables us to become pure so that we can have communion with Him. Indeed, it is by His Spirit living within given through the resurrection which caps the plan. Only, when we live within the capped plan of God {like a bolt with two caps on it} can we be sure that He has given the plan, will make the intention, and provide for the outcome.

And we find ourselves somewhere in between the plan and the outcome.

On a Wing and a Prayer is the difference between knowing where you want to be. It is the door between here and there, now and whenever.

For we see in a mirror dimly now, but in time, we will see clearly. In time we will know truly, without a doubt.

But, for now we are not sure.

And what is the difference between being not sure and knowing without a doubt something is true.

It is the same thing which brings you through to that place which, up until now, you only saw in a dream.

We cannot manufacture it because we do not have the building products for such a place.

It is impossible to fake belief in something which we hold to be false. Others know.

And every once in a while, in a field full of yellow daisies, there will be a purple one.

It is someone who stands out affirming that something is true. But, we argue, it is not tried so how do we know it is true?

God does not fabricate from that which already exists: He creates new from not.

And every once in a while, He puts it into someone's heart to see the finished product before it's built. That individual can see an arm grown where only a stub now stands.

That person can see a bridge where there is a chasm between.

Oh, we say, 'Certainly, you are but a dreamer. It has never been done before.'

And, isn't that what a dreamer does: peek through a dark place to see a picture of something which does not {yet} exist?

A dreamer sees a light that shines onto the back of his imagination revealing things not seen by the physical eye. He peeks into a place, just like peeking through a keyhole, to see things happen which aren't {yet].

Is the dream true or not?

Faith is what gives us spiritual eyes to see the dreams of God and it is His grace which pulls our belief through the keyhole; then we follow carried by His power.

It is said, that 'It is harder for a camel to get through the eye of a needle than a rich man to enter into the Kingdom of God.'

And, you say, why is this?

I ascertain that we refuse to let go of the things which we carry; we hang onto the provisions of this world and refuse to rely on that which comes from above. When we are clinging to the 'here and now', we cannot focus on the 'then and there'.

You see, Jesus told the rich man to give away all of his riches and come and follow Him. Did He mean that the man would be poor? Certainly. You see we can only understand the poor 'in spirit' when we become as they are. We can only understand the meek when we become as they. We can only understand the humility of Jesus when we become humble. He wants us to become 'poor' in this world that we may understand heavenly riches.

Only when we are willing to leave the things of the world behind, will we be able to see clearly the things of the Kingdom of God.

This book is about looking to the promises of God, then getting there. It is about being threaded from the place where you are to the place where God intends you to be. If, indeed He has a plan for your life, then He also has a place where He wants you to end up. I will outline the difference between your calling, being anointed, training and being given a mission that is on God's heart.

This book is one of the books in a series of Steps in the Garden.

The first book, Coriantá teaches about the love of God, the next book, Tomaseña, shows you how to listen to His voice. The following book, Katísha, helps you to understand the difference between the kingdom of Satan, the World, the flesh and the Kingdom of God. Miracles', book four, shows us that when we learn to listen to God, He will tell us who He is and then He will tell us who we are. Only then, can we be- come one who reflects Him accurately. The next book, Sinactía, deals with the effects of sin; past, present and future. Then there's one book on receiving your gifts from God, Camezía The next book demonstrates how to share your gifts with others, Festevía. Then, we come to this book, which connects these elements, threading you through the purpose using the provision to the promise. You can read about them in the back of this book or on-line at www.gloryboundpublishing.com.

Enjoy On a Wing and a Prayer
I pray that you may be threaded through the hands of God to the place of His dreams. Sheri Hauser

Contents

A letter from the author.

I.	Threads from Heaven	11
II.	Homespun Teaching	29
III.	Spools of Wisdom	49
IV.	Woven Promises	67
V.	Tapestry of Faith	85

Caëfa   107

Chapter 1

Threads from Heaven

His Pearl

With sincerity I have sought thee, Dear Lord.
Heart fixed on crossing Your ford.
Intent on the desire of Yours.
Sweat oozing from my pores,
Pour into my life, edge me about with Your knife.
Bring me to Your waterfall.
The world only gives me gall.

Onto Your chest, let me rest my head.
Hear Your heartbeat, free from dread.
Spirit of love, Spirit of truth
Come to the old, come to the youth.

Bring Salvation and breathe to life us.
Winds of mercy, true light be bright.
Wisp of voice, let us rejoice.

In You alone, in You.
Oh, Father, Son and Spirit divine billow my soul,
become someone mine.
I give You my heart, my life into Your hands.

Thread Your provision, fulfill Your plans.
Be My desire, light a Holy fire
Within, without amidst Around, among, instead.

And, provide for my delight, dear Lord.
For, I know that is truly You, to give when it's night.
To provide what is true,
I love You, I love You.

In thee, do I trust.
I love You, I love You, and I ask You, You Must.
Bring life to Your word, life to Your voice.
Constraint to the devil, I give You the choice.
Become my desire, my heart I give.
I give You my life, set me apart to live.

With sincerity of heart, I have sought thee,
meet me at my own.

Be free, My love,
in thee. It's Me,
My dove, it's Me
With glee, My sweet, I free thee to love
only Me. Me in thee, and thee in Me.
A mix a mingle of wine and water,
the fruit of your hands and the provision brought by Me
declare My love, sent from above.

From a Father to a girl, to Him, His only pearl.
For, the shell has been opened, the treasure released.
The pearl of great price, my daughter,
the Church My precious Child is now
to receive. Mounds and mounds of
love; I have piles.
Pearls of wisdom, riches of light.
Gems of insight, come through the night.

Once held within a shell, you have been opened.
Now, face the light you hope in.
Hope within to shine without.
Pearls of knowledge, release from doubt.
Everlasting trust in a Father's love,
Eternal promises from God above.

Give Me your heart, I give it true.
Give Me your life, I gave Mine for you.
And, the gift never stops, because the giver,
He lives. Lives on eternal, giving to live.

A Memorial Day

    The message doesn't change because the environment changes. It's the same, only the target is different. Change your hair to meet the target. It does. Watch.

    When I go to speak to the younger generation, I need to dress like the role that I am playing. I need to wear the hippie stuff that I already have. I can make my hair to match because it is flexible. I will be 'cool' if I put some colors and braids in it. It's OK if they respond to me like a 'madam' because at least they will listen. They are tired of the stereo types of Christians that they see on TV in suits and coats all glimmered up. They can't connect with these types. Show them your true self; show them that you are a revolutionist at heart; so am I. I started the biggest revolution in history, remember. It shouldn't be strange that you take after Me.

    I have been trying to put this whole thing together and it's about to come together. It will meet its goals and wrap around the purpose because we all have dreams, but it is truly different when we rely on God to make them what He wants them to be.

    These are His dreams that I have been following, so He is going to make the goals wrap around their purposes. I forgot to ask Him the purpose. What is Your purpose, Dear Lord?

My purpose is to show my children my love. I want to caress their forehead at night and let them know it's me. I have been coming to their beds at night and they don't know it's me. As a Father, I want them to realize it's me. You know, now blab.

When God calls me and I stop and turn around, it makes the dream to move; local becomes afar. It takes on a personal touch and moves the dream to another level. Once we grab hold of the dream, we can always come back to it. It is ours and we own it by virtue of reaching out and grasping those golden threads of light.

As I have grasped hold of the aspect of interpreting dreams, then they have touched to where I can grab them. If I never wrote them down, then I would not have known the content. But, it is more than that… from writing them down to believing that they are from God and wanting to obey the message. It is another level of faith to believe that the message is from Him. We can write the message, but to believe it is from Him is different. And, when we believe it's from Him, then what do we do? We must make a decision. There is a crossroads that happens. Do we ignore the dream, or try to make sense of it and learn what the message means to us?

Given and taken to under the authority of Himself.

God is the one who gives the dreams and it is under His authority that they go out to those for whom they are intended. Satan has no authority to interrupt messages from God. We misunderstand demons in our dreams as being from the Devil. It is God telling us that they are there: He shows them to us in a form that we can see. They were there all the time around us, only when we have a dream and they are there, we can't deny it any longer.

Glory Pass

His Glory passes where yours stops.

Wisdom

Wisdom: think about her as your mother. She doesn't demand attention, but is grateful when you do. There is a chair of wisdom where we become filled, drilled, and enameled. Like cavities in teeth, we climb into our chair and let Him work on us in the areas of our lives that need help. And, He fills the cavities of our heart with gold. He drills out the old stuff; that which brings us rottenness and decay to our soul, then, He fills with pure promises and truth.

Wisdom from on high, from the hand of the master craftsman, it comes. And, we know we have made our appointment because we leave looking different; cleaned and filled, pressed, and sealed, covered with His provision because He insures His plans. The bridge needed to be built before anyone could walk across it. It is a bridge of understanding God's voice through dreams.

The power point press is when I give you a dream, then lead you through it. You move from dream to reality by following the truth: Me.

We become like a needle point picture when we press through the place where He shows us in a dream. He shows the place that we need to enter, and it makes the colors in the picture make sense. We begin to understand the purpose of our existence. Then, when we stand back, we can see the canvas of our life that is being woven.

And, we have two apartments. There are two places that we rent.

There is one we receive and one we show others. We can get one refurbished, but chances are it will need some stuff. And, they thought because I lived on the high end of town, that mine was fancy. On the contrary, it was a low rent flat that cost around sixty dollars that was gutted and repaired; redone. Then, I added a garden space behind this condominium to grow just the things I need. Now, they want me to talk about it.

They will see the products that I have in my hand and think that I live on the high end of town. I need to tell them that I actually came to God poor and He is the one that changed me. I was like an old rental property; I just resold my life to Him and let Him gut me out. He is the one that made the conversion in the place. He is the one that led the refurbishing project. I still don't own anything; all I have is His. The one that I show others looks different because I have been changed.

The outside is the same except that I have added a garden. I have learned how to grow in the garden of His love. And, now He gives me the seeds that I need to grow exactly what fits well within my soil and the environment of my area. I take no credit for the renewal project. It was His idea.

I am on a ranch owned by another and need to get ready to go to testify at court. I am part of the evidence against someone. I simply need to tell the truth. Still, I need to get ready the rest of the way. My hair is kind of flat. I go to the yard and decide to drive the pickup truck around. The problem is that I have a very hard time stopping. The truck is old and the brakes are even older. It won't stop. By the time I get it stopped, I uproot a palm tree. But, I fix it and replant some other seedlings along the way.

I am in a place where seedlings are grown and soil is stored, and babies are born. It is a happy place full of life with lots of action.

Many will spring to life and many seeds of the words of God will burst forth inside of the right hearts that are ready to receive them.

It is time for me to testify about what God has said. He is going to put me on the stage and display me to others. It is me that is the display because I have followed the dreams to writing the books and gone to the end of the bridge. Because, you can talk a lot about how God speaks in dreams, but to show them, is another story. It takes the message to another level. They believe because they will see the demonstration of grace within my life. What I am about to do is rebut the lies of the enemy. And, it will be easy because I have the truth.

Like a notebook tucked under my arm, I am ready with the testimony. I needed to write the testimony down to be ready to show it to others.

I need to get ready the rest of the way. My hair is flat. My head is not lifted. God is saying that He is the one who lifts my head and He wants it to be lifted before I am ready to face others. Not only am I to take comb to my hair, but to come to Him and let my head be lifted. Within the field that He has put me in, I climb into the old pick-up.

There is a way that I have been picked-up over and over. And, He is calling me to do it. Climb into praise and worship and allow my head to be raised by Him. The problem is that when I enter His courts of praise, I don't know how to stop. As the praise has been directed by Him, I never learned how to stop it. How could I expect to, now. It turns palms upward when I enter this old area of praise. Good idea.

Palms need to be turned up and the old area of praise needs to be uprooted and restored. Others will learn how to praise as well.

God gave me the job of writing and now He is calling me to do another job. I didn't direct the writing, so I am going to have a hard time stopping.

The gardener comes along and shows me how to do things right.

There are bags of planting soil piled high ready to use, but because he wasn't there alongside of me at the time, I use some of the wrong soil. He says that it's not a big deal. It's just picky stuff and a matter of a few fibers, but now that I know the difference, next time I will be more careful.

I am surrounded by so much tender writings that I am not sure how to put them all together. But, that's OK. I may have made some minor mistakes in the first books; they will get better as I learn how to have Jesus as my constant companion. He will show me the soils of the hearts and which to plant where. There is a difference in the threads of soils that is minor, but important. The dreams are different and before I clumped them together because I didn't know any better, but He will continue to teach me the differences between them.

I go to the barn and the daughter is delivering one newborn after another.

Now I need to get ready to testify. I am rushed to fix my hair. I have three ways I can fix it. (modern, daily and high style depending on the audience.)

There are three ways for my head to be lifted. I can lift it to Him, let Him come to me and allow others to lift me. There is no room in this story to elevate my own head.

It was such a daredevil stunt that He pulled off. Many thought He determined to ride right over the hills and into the cliff, but, I watched and He was just having fun. Then, I end up in the water swimming with the Father. He knows I am going to be short in time, yet He stalls me with swimming. Is not intimacy along the way, important? I need to fix my hair along the way. I just need to do it.

It was a daredevil stunt that God led to have me write so much in such a short time. And, didn't I dare Him? Yes I did. And, Yes, He did above and beyond all I could have imagined. And, is it time to praise Him? Of course. And, do I need company to do it with? Of course not, dear Lord. As I pause and praise You, Amen. Don't forget to pause for a kiss.

I am afraid to open my eyes in my new state because I sense then it will be ugly. It just feels ugly, but it's not. It's just on the other side. And, we will get all that we need to be there on time because Karna and I are in the center of the walk with the baby.

Indeed, I am worried about what is on the other side because there are still 4000 books in my garage, soon to be 14000 books. And, I have a continuing stack of bills that is much bigger than the books. Not to mention, I have committed myself to even more by offering jobs to individuals when I have no idea where their salary is to come from. It could be ugly. But, this dream gives me hope in that, I am soon on the other side and all we need is there. I must not forget that this walk includes my sister, Karna.

I renew my old lease to commemorate Memorial Day. The books are new answers of one I honor and how he killed the old Him and the old man and revealed them both. Now we stand tall for the Army of God.

God killed the old image I had of Him, as well as my old nature, so it should not be odd that I respond to a new God with a new self.

As He has risen, so have I. Memorial Day is to honor those who have died in the service of their country. And, indeed we have. He has died and I have. We both are to be honored today because we have given our all for the service of His Army; The Kingdom of God.

At this store the hours are 'come as you are.' There is something new. They thought that they had to change before they came, but not this place. He will refurbish you in and out and tend your flower beds. Refurbishes and upkeeps by the management are included in one price, the purchase of your soul and when you ask.

Most businesses only allow you to visit at specific hours of their convenience, but with this business, He is open all of the time. God is open to speaking to us all of the time and we can speak to Him all the time. And, this is a come as you are business. We come as we are. We do not need to wear special clothes to do His business. He changes us to meet what He needs. He has purchased the opportunity to freely talk with us any time. We need to open the channel to make it a two-way conversation.

And, now I will testify. There are only a few minor things to be done. I brought my outfit, but I see that my shoes are best from Karna's stuff. They match nearly perfect. They are a little lighter than the rest but look wonderful. The lace matches with the shoes and the purse. I have the purse and she lends me the shoes to wear. It makes a very elegant outfit; a top notch presentation.

It is best to put on the face of lightheartedness, like the one displayed in the art of Karna's within the book. God wants to demonstrate His light heart.

I just need to make a change from planting and tending the growth to the testimonial presentation. It's hard to put the brakes on something that I really never learned to drive.

My testimony is crucial. To tell the truth is all I need to do. It's easy because all I have is the truth.

I am not planting and tending but telling about me. It's what I am supposed to do: Lighthearted conversation about dreams and how He taught me to interpret them.

Get ready to hydrate. It's a wonder they have never seen before: Clarity to the vision through the presence and power of God.

Get ready for the water to pour out. God will pour out His Spirit in such a way that they will see clearly how it all fits together. He will show His presence to them and in doing that He will show His power. The same tingles that individuals feel, all who hear your voice will feel because I will confirm the truth in their own spirits. It's a spiritual clap. I have given all a spirit to enable them to understand Me, yet it needs to be woken up. It's not that they don't want to wake up, but it's that they can't. I will shout at them. It's just a crack of light that leads them to the door. It's their choice. But, hey never had it before now.

When she comes into the room, she cleans. It's a clean sweep of the Holy Spirit. The base to the pole needed washing.

As I go to interviews, I will ask God what He wants me to say and as for the Holy Spirit to help. I will clean up on the enemy's dirt related to dreams. It will be gone in an instant when the washing of the truth comes. The water washes as it comes. The base of what holds the truth needed washing, through the forgiveness for sin. That is what made it all to happen. The door has been closed because of the thickness of the veil of sin in our lives. When I was willing to work through the veil of sin, then it tore down the partition that separated the truth from us over the element of God's voice in dreams.

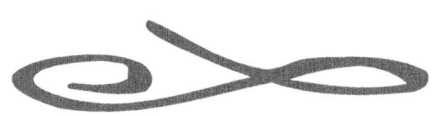

Threads of God's Voice: A Dream

They all left and I cleaned the house. I found what gathers the threads that others had long since forgotten about. No one was left in the church to pray. I was alone day after day. As I sought God fervently and personally, He met me. He gave me the threads of His wisdom.

Then, He gave me a vacuum cleaner. He showed me how to gather them together. He gave me the ability to gather the threads of His voice within dreams. It was in the carpet that I found it as I lay face down worshiping My Father. And, after I had gathered the threads of

His voice, I stared at them in wonder, for I didn't know what to do with them.

So, I asked the one who had given them to me. Then, He gave me understanding to follow the threads back to their origination: His carpet. Those threads came from His place. I followed the path that was laid out for me along the road. That part was easy. It just ran parallel to the road. The challenge was getting the door open to enter into the place where the threads came from, but once I did, I left it ajar for others. Just as I finish the cleanup, they come home towing their old vehicle. I have paid my brother's way by my work. Now he can come. Everywhere I turn there are more doors that simply need to be opened. A door is no hindrance. It just needs to be passed through.

Threads of Praise

Praise You Father of love
Praise You Heavenly Lord, above.
Holy Spirit, I lift my adoration to You
On the wings of the Dove, You flew.
Praise You Father of Love
Amazing grace sent from above
Thread Your love through my heart.
Come and stay, never depart.
God of mercy, God of love
Praise to You from below to above

Life Dreams and Visions

A dream is what God puts in our heart as the goal, while the vision is how we will reach it. The dream is the cloud, while the vision is the ladder that leads to it. Many times, we will have the dream long before we understand how to get there.

The steps will be set before us one by one after we get the dream firmly planted in our heart. A dream is in the heart, and a vision is in the brain because a dream is given at night, whereas a vision is given in the daytime. The work is done during the light, so the vision pertains to 'what to do', while the dream pertains to 'why'.

When we have a goal, then we need steps to reaching it. The steps are not a dream, but ways to get toward the fulfillment of the dream. Often, we are confused about the difference between the dream and the vision. The dream never changes, but the vision depends on our vantage point. Perhaps we see things differently today than we saw them before because our knowledge base has expanded.

For example, if I have a dream of helping others to hear the voice of God through the interpretation of their own dreams, then the vision of how to carry out that dream changes along the way. Maybe at one time I share through written words, and another through a talk show.

The dream becomes the destination and the vision becomes the vehicle to get us there. Whichever hill we happen to be on is the one where we will be seeing the circumstances through. Do we see through our own eyes or the eyes of another?

Perhaps we have a dream but are relying on someone else to fulfill it. We may have our own dream, but someone else's vision. Certainly, we will trip when we don't see where our own feet are.

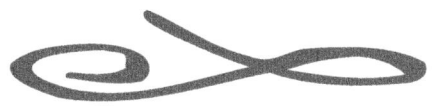

Here's a testimony so you can see what I mean:

Miracle Anointing

I received anointing for miracles. With that came a vision of a huge wishbone. What God showed me was that often we 'wish' for things and, like children tugging on a wish bone we only hope to receive a large share of what we hope for. We are settling for dry bones. Dry bones have no life and they are not of God. They don't demonstrate the character of God.

What He did was put a large wish bone into my hand, and then show me how to wrap the bone around itself until it 'snapped'. What happened when the power of God 'snapped' the hope to life. Then, I gave Him the pile of dry bones to revive- and like Ezekiel – I spoke to the dry bones and they came to life.

So, I received anointing to do miracles of opening hearing for those who are deaf, the eyes of those who are blind, raising the dead, and a couple of others which I cannot remember at this time.

As confirmation of the gifting, He gave me two gold crowns.
{Actually, two crowns in my mouth turned to gold which were not gold before.} This was given on my second {two-th} birthday of my company Glory Bound Books Ltd. He had given me words about 'cutting my teeth' in business the day before, then when He gave me the vision and the anointing, He gave me the two gold crowns. It was 'like' a business birthday present. I'm wondering what He will give on my third birthday. I really don't want a mouth full of gold crowns.

January 29th 2007

Ferrying Gifts

The Dream:
Certainly, we are going touring. I arrive just as mom is getting off the ferry. It is an ocean-going ferry which will sail a great distance. She says that I am to go now because now is the time to go. So, she yells at the Chinese captain to wait and he holds the boat while I run aboard. I tell her I have no ticket. They gave me no ticket when I paid for my fare as I left the last ride, but she said that they only gave her a ladies' watch. Then she gives me a small piece of rope to give to the captain as a present. On this ride you get on by your word. I run aboard. I will sit with the captain and keep him company. He is happy to have company.

No other people are aboard this ride except a family that watches dogs for others. I'm thinking that I don't want to get attacked by those dogs, but as they go by, they are more interested in one another than me. They are a mixed breed leashed by the one who has control over them. They roam the ship on the mountain in the center.

So, I give the little rope to the captain. It is so versatile that he can use it to attach anything he wants to his ferry. He could even tie onto the dock for a while if he wants.

Interpretation:
This shipment of grace isn't driven by God from the front. Prayer is what drives the kingdom of God. This is the place where others walk for others. There are some that you will find on this mountain of prayer which crosses over to foreign countries who have no gifts of their own. They accept responsibility for that which isn't theirs and receive payment for it.

Theirs is a different task because they are hirelings being pulled along by a mixture generated by the needs of those who sent them. But they walk without a purpose of their own and they have no relationship with the Captain of the ship.

They are too busy trying to control the needs of their supporters to spend time with the captain of the ship. They have no presentation of their own and they have no gifts, but handle other's pet projects.

They have been sent to represent others. Missionaries are on a mission generated by individual groups. What they have done is string them all together and attempt to fulfill all of their purposes at the same time.

These are 'families' who gather support from several Churches, then go to foreign countries. The problem is that their mission isn't to please their Father, but all the Churches who pay their way. There is no offspring from their walk; no fruit from their tree because there can't be. It's like a German Shepherd trying to breed with a fox terrier. When they attempt to combine the directive for mission from one Church with the other, this group of 'missionaries' are scary because their vision is not their own, so their purposes are undefined. Like a deformed baby, the purpose is frightening, and he can never breathe on his own.

Hold the Vine

Father, make me a cup.
Not an ordinary cup, but a communion cup.
One filled with fruity flavor kept until the right season
and released on time.
Make me suitable to be held in Your hand
and freely offered to others.

Keyhole

The string threads through the keyhole in the paper.

I punch the hole in the paper that provides the place where the provision is threaded through.

I am the keyhole that He will thread the provision through. He is the key that unlocks the door: the only reason to rush the season.

Father, I am sorry. Forgive me for my selfishness.

In my desire to be comfortable within Your provision, I have forgotten the purpose.

Emancipation Declaration

Heard from on High, herald of an angel
Hark, a spark from beyond heard from on High
Elevation collaboration emancipation declaration.
Heard from on High, He gives through a kit
From afar came the light, bright light, night light, His light, sight light.
Herald of an angel, heard from on High.
Palacious prescriptions, precious presence without
He brings to within. Presents from a King, intentions of a physician, written inside. From without, He brings within, His palace to our house, and makes it His own.

Crafts

The Dream:
The first time I got into the high flying craft, it was hard. I nearly tipped it over. My daughter helped me a lot. The second time I just said, "Scoot over."

I wanted to see if I could do it, myself. And, I did it! It was a wonderful success. Certainly, it was exercise. By exercise I can discern where I am to where I need to be and get there. The in between spot is not as uncomfortable as it was before. Faith.

Interpretation:
When I began to understand dreams and hearing the voice of God, I received a lot of help from those mature in the Holy Spirit at Church.

{The daughter}. I was very inept at driving the vehicle which God had given me and looked a lot like a high School driver with her first driving lesson. The first dream took me about a month to interpret. But, I was persistent in trying to hear God's voice for myself through the spirit of prophecy, interpretation of tongues and understanding dreams and visions. Like someone exercising for a meet, I continued to try, exercising my spirit to teach it how to become sensitive to the things of God.

At first, I was very unsure that I was hearing the voice of God when He spoke to me. But, as I stepped out {of the boat} in faith attempting to {walk on water} believe that God could speak to my spirit and I would, at some point, be able to understand, I became more and more sure of my footing. I learned how to step out on faith believing God's voice.

Beneficial to God

Beneficial is your dedication to Me. For, within the scope of your practice, I exercise. By your hand, I exercise My will to bring about My provision.

Unobstructed Breathing

The Dream:
The church wants to be able to breathe on her own, so I have removed the obstruction from her throat. Now, she will be able to. I took her off the ventilator. I removed the manual breathing tube. Man no longer controls her air. I will give her air, myself.

Interpretation:
I am an Intensive Care Nurse and work with patients who are on ventilators. We put them on breathing machines when they cannot breathe on their own. When they have surgery and are put into a deep sleep, they use breathing machines to keep them aerated during the surgery. If people come into the hospital with any kind of respiratory distress, such as Asthma, then we put them on a breathing machine.

What the breathing machine does is deliver man-made breaths when the individual cannot breathe on his own. It consists of a 'breathing tube' which is put down their throat into their lungs, then it is attached to a machine which delivers a specific amount of oxygen at a timed rate and volume. The doctor decides how much based on the size of the patient and the treatment that is needed.

I needed to give the background information related to the breathing machine for those who don't understand about them so that they will see the correlation between the man-made breaths and someone who can breathe on his own. Babies, as soon as they are born, take their first breath. All babies breathe on their own {unless there is a problem}. And, we continue to breathe on our own until the breath stops and we pass onto another world. That is the circle of life.

The correlation with the dream is that the Church has a 'breathing tube' which it doesn't need. If a person can breathe on their own, he doesn't need a ventilator to help him to breathe. The message of the dream is that the Church can breathe on its own. What that means is that we do not need someone to control what we inhale. God wants to give us our own air. The Holy Spirit is called the 'breath' of God. He wants to give us His breath without man-made machinery. We do not need automated teaching methods to understand the God's voice.

In the dream, I remove the tube, which could be a help, but in this case, has become an obstruction to the individual breathing on his own.

So I will do it:
Father, I pray that You will free the Church to breathe on its own. Remove anything which stands in the path of them receiving all You have. Become their inspiration. Amen

---

God's Oreo

I think that if there was a chocolate
bar called understanding, it would be
cream filling sandwiched between
two cookies. For, God puts us
in the palm of His hand.
He threads His fingers between ours
and pulls us close to
Himself.
Then,
He
Covers
us with His other.
*Father, please
fill us with
understanding
of Your love. Thread
Your fingers through ours and pull us in*

Chapter 2

Homespun Teaching

Will you Still Love Me, Then?

Will you still love Me
after you are tried, pressed
and put down by the world? Will
you still love me if they hate you?
Because you stand for what they hate.
You know that, don't you? They view My
wisdom as foolish, silly, and stupid. The world
tries to reason My existence right out of their whole
existence. There is philosophy and science. There is love
of money
and pride.
Love of themselves is the worst of all. What you are
preaching is like combing the hair on a dog backwards.
It is not going to feel good to everyone. Oh, I know
it feels good to you. And, I know you have
supporters. I put them there. But, there
are many who won't want their hair
combed backwards because
it exposes things in their

Will You Still Love Me? (Cont.)

lives that they have covered up. Warts, tics, and
cancer of matted flesh that they have tucked
into the folds of fur and fat. Then, you come
along with the message of light and your
fancy comb, just like a hairdresser.
Many won't come. Many won't pay.
Many will sneer. Still more will be
jealous of you. Everything
about you. Because you
resemble Me.
Remember,
they hated Me
first. Will you still love Me,
then? Oh, Lord. You know
my heart. I pray for you to
strengthen our cords
of love.
Those cords; make
them gold threads
wrapped in diamonds.
I need some strong tensile
strength, here Lord. OK?
Attach them;
my heart to yours and I give the
responsibility to you. Keep me there. OK? Thanks.

Tools on our Knees

The Dream*:*
When I got down on my knees, I found all sorts of tools for sewing. Mending broken hearts, repairing connections between people and God, sewing threads of God's love and grace. There are tools for managing threads.

Interpretation:
When the carpet is rolled back, things are revealed that tear garments apart. Under the threads we have tools that help to take things apart. For, hidden within our own prayer life are options to cut the way things seem. We have the ability to reveal the true needs in prayer when we become fervent. The real needs need to be revealed.

We need to use prayer to cut away the layers of padding that have been laid over the foundation. The foundation of prayer cuts to the heart of everything. Many times, we have fluff padded what is important. God isn't interested in the fluff of prayer. He is concerned with the true needs, cut to the heart, tear away the seams of the Devil.

Pray in Flags

If you pray, Sing Gods request in tongues.
For when you pray for God to sing, He will
send in His flags.
He will send His purpose, through His people
As they move toward the needs of those in need.
To have
God
sing to
them, bring
flags and leave them
in the aisles Fabrics. Pass them out
Let the people elevate them in honor to God.

A Model in the Way

The Dream:
On this cruise ship when you go up the gang plank, you enter another world that you never knew existed. All the places are blue, advertising my blue heart for the children. Like the others, when you press against My face, it opens. In your dreams, you press with a writer.

Others are certain to come with you.

With this shipment of grace, when you enter into the place where God is the captain, you enter into another world: His. All of the places are blue. It is His cord on blue; where He sings His blue heart chords. He has sandwiched His bread, His meat and a Holy cheese. For, it is a meeting of His Holiness, and fresh bread from heaven. Coriantá is an advertisement for God's true-blue heart. {See the book Glory Bound Books Ltd.} As I have pressed against His face, He has left His imprint on me. His imprint on me has led to interpreting dreams using the spiritual gifts that He has given with His presence.

He says within this dream that others are certain to come with me. God says that He will reveal Himself to whosoever He wills, but this book has twisted His arm in a special way because within it is the ability for Him to reveal Himself any way He wants. He knows each of our houses and knows what we need. He outlines the areas we need and fills in the rest with things that are written within the book. He outlines the parameter of their need and fills it with grace. It is just like the poetry shapes in that He draws the shape then pours the words into it. {Like on the previous page.} He has drawn out His parameters of communion with each of us and pours into it what we need. He walks the rails of our lives with us, setting us on whatever track we need to be on.

And when they tried to go on the train, they saw it had been turned into a model. We took ours tours in my bathrobe and I never could get them to say which team I was on. I was afraid nobody wanted me. Just because I am not young doesn't mean I don't want to play. There is not conductor to this train. It's a model. We all have our own contacts.

And, when they try to read the book from my perspective, they will see that it is impossible because God will begin to speak to them personally. As He spoke to me in my bathrobe, He will speak to them, as well.

*I have wanted to become part of the team, but I am a revolutionary. I am the one that helps to draw the lines, like working with the umpire. The truth is that I am not like them, because I am the one who was given the stuff to start with. As I have teamed up with Him, He has become My teammate. I have worried that others won't accept me as part of the team, but God is saying that **what He has given me is a model for teamwork** He has given me the guidelines for the service ministries with Him and others.*

No wonder they didn't want me on their team. Who would pass out the parameters of the field if I was with them? For, I am one who surveys the whole field. He has placed the whistle in my hand to call them to the fields that they are intended to be in. {I have the gift of anointing: I can tell others what their anointing is.}

God is putting me in with those in the field who are having fun. I could do that, too, if I am called to. Just because I am old, doesn't mean that I don't know how to enjoy life.

I started out wanting to be part of the team, but nobody would choose me. As much of a heart I had for prayer, they were reluctant to let me become part of their program. My life was cluttered with broken promises of ministry. What was a log in my eye, I tried to overcome? I had tried to follow their training programs, but they didn't work, so I took off on my own.

I followed my need for healing of the log that was in my eye. God showed me the deceptive place of the enemy, and I avoided it. I avoided the deception within the teaching that God was giving me. Yet the log continued to be there. I had a grudge against those who had passed me over and chosen others for positions of authority. I have tried to get over it but have been unable to.

Interpretation:

I have seen where their teachings were blatantly wrong. It got to the point where the teaching that I was given was so divergent from what they had told me, that it became like splinters in my feet. Even though I had written the program I could no longer even bare to touch it. Certainly, that was not the way to go. The program just stood in my path of being healed and restored.

And, I have walked with that log, like it was huge. That training model was nothing but a huge splinter in my eye. It is a splinter that becomes a log making healing impassable because the model impedes what we need on the other side. And, in the dream, the model train is driving off a cliff. I believe this dream is telling me that I have driven conventional programs of teaching others how to hear the voice of God over a cliff. These models don't work because that is what they are: scaled down versions of the truth. They are not the truth, but a picture of it. And they are not the picture that we individually need. God wants to give us our own model: Him. Jesus is our model.

This model won't hold my weight. It isn't strong enough. It also impedes my ability to get to the other side of where I need to be. It stands in the way of progress. It is like a log in the road that blocks our way to where God needs for us to go. It looks down on people. It exalts itself above others. Nobody seems to notice that it is made from a log. It makes you wonder if the program wasn't written by someone who was slighted by not getting a position of authority within their church. Did they, then build their own model for teaching and sell it to others?

The train is the vehicle that carries the resources. The train is what goes down the track toward the destination. Wisdom is our trainer.

The power of God provides the engine that moves the train down the track that God has intended for us. If the wisdom of God is our train and it is empowered by the Holy Spirit moving along the path set out by God, then it is sturdy. The train in the dream was not on a track but built out of a log. It was made of sacrifices of men, forged from what their hands had made.

It was not built to handle the weight of others. Sacrifice and commitment to a program are not strong enough to keep others on track.

In the dream, the train is headed for a cliff. If we don't fall through, fall out, we will certainly fall over what the training program has to offer. There is no way around, over or through a training built on the platform of sacrifice. We will give our time, money and self to accomplish its goals, yet it does not give us relief from the things that are blocking our path. It does not shed light on our individual needs and show us how to avoid dangers.

Programs of self-sacrifice that try to put us on track are a flimsy excuse for the real thing. The training will fall through the minute we attempt to put some weight on it. When testing comes, the matrix of it will crumble. The problem is that the purpose does not meet the goal because the purpose of the writer was different from yours. It may have met his goal, but it doesn't meet yours. If you pick a plan because you like the goal, then there will be problems because the plan was written from the standpoint of the one who met his goal. For instance, if the goal was to 'become mature in prayer for the Church' then the individual started out on a path which ended up with the goal being met. That person was in a specific place at a certain time in his life and God worked with him to bring him to the place of his desire.

The problem is that we are not at the same place that he was when he wrote the training program. In essence, he was in New Jersey while we are in San Diego. If we try to follow a map to Tennessee that has directions leading from New Jersey when we are in San Diego, then we will have problems. No amount of sacrifice, persistence, demon warfare, or following the directions explicitly will allow you to make this train be your trip from your take off point to another's destination.

In the dream, I try to push over the top of the log, and it doesn't work. And, the whole train is high up.

That is where it leads: to the train. You don't train them. The books lead them through your steps to the train, but through it. They aren't steps to train, but steps to get to the front of the train. I have met the engine of the train. It has been my training exercise.

Manifestation of Glory

The
glory
of God
won't come
when there isn't
anything to carry it in.
We are the containers who
carry the manifested glory of God.

Only when we become available can God's glory
be shown through our lives. We bare witness
of Him and demonstrate evidence of His glory.

Threaded through His Purity

Thread my soul through Your needle, Lord. I want to see life through Your eye.

The wind that whistles by your face is the same wind that I whistle. Why, then wouldn't it be the very breath I exhale? You have become My exhale: the outflow of My air. Because I am God purity flows in and purity flows out. I give you pure air. The world gives mixed elements. Oh, that you could stop breathing the air of the world and just breathe Mine!

Essence of purity of My Spirit.

That is why I put it within you. Don't you believe it? You don't understand what that means. My purity flows from within your lungs; your outflow has become mine because I have placed My purity within you. You don't have to worry about it, because you need nothing from the world.

That is why I call you flowers, because you have a fragrance unfamiliar to the world: fresh aroma. You are fresh air. It's the purity they lack.

Green Light at Work

The Dream:
Check the connection on the light to your patients, then, move on if the light turns green. A pause is not a stop, but merely a pause. Check for traffic before running into the road.

Interpretation:
When I come to my patients, I need to pause and check to see if there is a connection between me and them; them and God or all three of us. If there is, I move on full speed ahead. Just pause before going on; don't worry. I need to check to see if the green signal is from God, not the enemy. He may seek to run me down.

New in You

Over and above, around and through
in between me and you
To live is to die and to die is my gain
How I praise You, Lord, be my sustain

In between the times, the up and down, in and out
be what I need, I love you without a doubt.
You are my friend, come bless my heart
I need Your companionship, Lord, never depart.

Over and above, around and through
thread Your love between me and You.
Between the times of honor and doubt
Between the joys and the times when I am without

Give me grace, hope and love,
Thread your mercy, bring the Dove.
Weave through my character what is Your desire
Grant new beginnings that I may aspire

To become new through You, through and through

Levels of Preparedness

The Dream:
What I thought would be nice has turned into something very difficult. I signed up for a few classes, and then took a break because the family needed me. Now I can't remember where to go or what to do. I have forgotten the assignments. There is immense frustration because I am late without being prepared. When I try to rely on my friends, they let me down. I manage to find one class and walk in late. I never quite figure out what they are doing to follow along.

Their books look vaguely familiar. This is a problem. Certainly, there is no way to fake knowing what to do at the right times. Either you are prepared or not. Then, I am not sure if I have another class or not and as I leave, I walk across people sleeping in beds. They have already gone to bed and I am still trying to find my next class to finish them. There is no other way out of this educational place than to walk through the same way I got in. I can't help it if it seems like I am late. They have simply gone to bed early. {Retired too soon.}

Interpretation:
Some set their mind to learn from God, yet become distracted by the needs of others. Some cannot discern between what God needs and what others need. Just because someone needs something, doesn't mean it is the voice of God calling to you. Many times, it is their voice which interrupts what God is trying to say. Then, when you finally return to what God was trying to say in the first place, you have forgotten the front of the message. It is like being left with the back half of the note; it is difficult to interpret it without the front of the note.

What this part of the dream is saying is that when God is teaching us a lesson, then we go off and 'help' people, when we return to the lesson, we will have a problem catching up.

If God is teaching us a lesson, we need to pay attention, grasp the material, then use it to help others. We must become prepared to serve others to do it God's way otherwise, we will do it our way because that is the only way we know how. To become prepared to serve in the Kingdom of God, we need to become trained, like attending College classes. There will be a certain amount of instructor time and some book work. We can plan on spending time with the Holy Spirit and the Word of God, then taking notes and studying them, so we can be ready for the test.

In the last part of this section, as I run off looking for my next class, I step over a lot of people who have gone to bed early. Some retire before it's time: they stop their training before it is time. The message is that when we set our mind to become trained by the Holy Spirit to serve God His way for His Kingdom purposes, we need to stick with the training and not become distracted by people's needs, and, we need to stay there until God declares that school is out for the day.

Second part of the dream:

And, I am not sure what I am supposed to do with the crying kid. I guess I have messed up something inadvertently as I rushed through in my attempt to find my classes. She became angry and her mom sent her to apologize. So, I will allow her to apologize for something I didn't even know about. It's the kind thing to do. She needs training, too.

Interpretation:

As you are going through your training by the Holy Spirit, sometimes, you may rush to your next class tripping over others in your excitement to get to the next class. As there are others nearby, they will be doing their own construction, like the child in the dream with the erector set. We may stumble along on our own path with such single focused desire that we fail to see others in our peripheral vision who might get in our way. We may inadvertently 'wound' them by something we say or don't say; something we do or don't do. The message of the dream says that we need to show kindness to those who may come to us saying they are sorry for being 'angry' over our interfering with their construction process. You see, because we are in the world together, we may bump into one another, causing some inadvertent damage to one another's construction projects. We need to be quick to forgive.

More Dream:

There are a few classes left and I need to push through to finish. My friend assumes I don't have her phone number because I ask for it.

{But, I do.} It is wrong to assume someone doesn't know something just because they look like they don't. I have it already; I just wanted to see if she would be willing to give it to me. I was testing her love.

Interpretation:

My dear friend, when I ask to be able to call you, it doesn't mean that I don't have the ability to call you on My own. What it means is that I want to be sure that you want to be called. I am looking for a mutual relationship of you calling Me and Me calling you. You see, we need to feel free to call one another, like friends, not like employee and employer. OK

Rope

I give you the rope
In You I hope
And cross we will
Your mission to fulfill.
Fill me full to do Your bill
It's a rope with a latch for you to attach
My heart to yours and open doors.

I give you the rope in You I hope.
It's just a small thing; that little piece of rope
But, I see now, how I became Your hope.
For with that rope attachments can become
Me to You becoming one.
Sharing with one another
The rope, the hope

Lighting the Candle

And I pray for this light, Father, Son and Holy Ghost
I pray to the choirs of heavenly Host
Remove intent of evil, in Jesus Mighty Name
Make the light bring You fame
not me.
Honor and glory, praise and laud
I praise Your Heavenly Name above Names, Almighty God

And, I pray for this light, Father, Son and Holy Ghost
Thread Your mercy and grace. In Your love may I boast
Eternal praise, earthly spirits raised high to You
Oh Heavenly Father, see me on through
To the place of Your intention.

And, I pray for this light. Bring Your sight
Go to the cracks of our despair, the corners of our pain
Crush our enemies, be our gain.
As we cling to Your honor above our own
Father, Son, Holy Ghost, come take the throne.

Fill this place, I pray today
Come to stay

And, pray for this light, Oh Lovely One
Dove of Peace, Prince of the Morning,
You who sets the colors in the bow
May they come to remember: come to know
It is You alone, and no one else who draws in the sky with His finger
Numbers the stars, counts the sand, yet by my side does linger.

Oh Prince of the Dawn, One who arises before I get up
Come to this place. Come join in my cup.
I have laid out the table, adorned it with a cloth
Embroidered the edge and showed no sloth
Working day and night, I have entered into Your field
demonstrating the gifts of the Spirit; Showing how to yield.

Oh, Holy Spirit come fill this place.
Let's be the first through the door. Come let's race.
Hand in hand let's sprint and take a peek
Look at the rooms. Play hide and seek.

Oh, Friend of Mine, I love You so
Only You know
Oh, Holy Spirit glow.

Shine, illuminate: bring the truth of Your Light
Come to this house set at the shore.
Oh Heavenly One, I need more
For, a light house is still without
Until the candle is lit.

And, you know I will, My love
I will come light this wick, My precious Dove
For the honor you show is not your own
The wind that billows your sails, I have blown.
Effervescent illumination, light into your soul
Colors of My Spirit given to show
I care.

For, I stand aloof, waiting to love those who know it not
They don't understand what they got.
The key is in their hand; I put it there long ago
And, only now I have sent you. We will show
that the key unlocks the door, opens the way and gives light
allowing the entrance of My word making everything bright.

And, you, wouldn't take 'No' for an answer
when the question continued to have a sign.
Would a God who loves, not want to align?
To be true to His word? You needed to know.

And, you came to the point where you had nothing left to loose.
You emptied your pockets, your hands and let Me choose
to give what was in Mine instead
You chose to learn how to be led.

Amazing insight, inspiration Divine has come
Because, you were the one
Who became willing.

You broke what you held precious; You gave your heart to Me.
Placed it in My hand and came to see the Me in thee.
And, thine is Mine. Fine wine dwelling in the triune.

And, I filled your cup with what you held out to Me.
The place of emptiness became the Me in thee.
And, we overflowed and continued to flow to today.
You see, I am here to stay.
Things eternal have replaced that which is not
That, My friend is what we got.

Eternal transversed a temporal place unknown in your own mind
Crossed over and came inside.
Now I can abide.
You in Me and Me in you.
We will show the glow
Now they know.

Running Along the Trail

If you drink ahead of time, you can move down the trail with greater speed because you are not thirsty, and you don't have to carry as much for along the way.

Because when you seek My face, I will show you your sin. You pray in hunger and walk toward your heart's desire repealing each sin as I show it to you.

Choosing our own Vehicles

I have it backwards. In my world I pick my own car. I go to the lot of my choosing and select from a variety of models based on my needs and the needs of my immediate family. The problem with my process is that I make myself responsible for it. By virtue of following my desires, I set myself up to pay for my own expenses. And, I can't afford my desires, so I take out a loan. I put myself in debt to someone else. And, maybe, I get my desires. More than likely, what I end up with is less than my hearts' desire. I take second best; what others think I can pay for, and I set myself up to meet their desires rather than mine. Their interest is what I pay for, and not one penny less.

The problem is that I started out to obtain the desires of my heart but ended up with a bill for someone else's. There is no honor in that; only pride for the one who railroaded me into a bill for something I didn't want. And, will this vehicle be able to meet my needs in the future? Probably not. It will become outdated, old and not trustworthy. It will breakdown when we need it most.

So, what will we do, then: Trade it in again for our heart's desire?

But our heart's desire is unknown to us. It is a mystery only to be opened by the one who created it. And, will we ever know what it is? I am not sure.

But, I do know that God is the one who knows better than anyone else. And, when we come to Him empty handed, He will hand us the key to the one He has set aside with our name engraved in the dash. And, it will meet our needs because He figures things the other direction. He sees the end of time and works backwards helping us to build a foundation of eternal worth so that He provides a framework that will last forever. In his auto zone we never trade in our vehicle for His service but continue to add accessories to the package. What we end up with in the end is more like a wonderful flying machine that is multipurpose. How could we possibly know what He would need for us to do ahead of time? We can't.

That is why it is better to ask Him to provide your car. He will pay for it, put it on His tab and hand you the keys. But, it's chauffeured, you know? There are no front seat drivers in His vehicles.

Being Stirred

Please respect the privacy of others. It is not your business to know their deepest secrets. What do you gain by knowing their private information? You won't understand. You aren't them. Their intimate issues are not for your curiosity. If you have known someone for a long time, you may assume you know why they are responding to God and others in a certain situation. You are wrong. You don't. It has not been given to us to know other's hearts.

That information is reserved for God. It's also, not our job to catch them when they fall. If God comes into a place and stirs a heart, let it stir. Tears don't cause pain. They are no indication of the issues in a heart.

They are simply a sign that a message has been transferred from the subconscious aspects to the conscious aspects. Perhaps it is a happy message of God's love and forgiveness.

Perhaps it is a call to change things previously left unattended. Maybe, it's a new burden that God has placed on their heart. For themselves or another. There is no way to know, without asking the person. But, it's important for us not to interfere with the stirring of the Holy Spirit because, maybe, it's a long message He is sending.

If we interrupt, then we will cause a break in the transmission. We need to stand back and pray for those we see stirred by the Holy Spirit. They really don't need Kleenex every time they cry. It's not necessary. The tears indicate a heart has been touched. That is a good thing.

We need not rush to comfort, console, encourage, or convict our brothers and sisters. Let them have their time with God in the midst of the congregation. It should be OK.

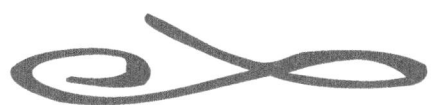

Imprinted Plans

You build with wood, plaster, and clay. I build with rock. You build with steel and marble. I build with rock.

You build your life with flexibility because you have to. You have no control over the provision.

Sure, you control the plans, but, dear friend many times they become like pages fed backwards to a printer. You feed the plan the best way you know how and insert he plan into your own provision; your printer, but somewhere between the plan and the provision there is a jam. Paper jam alert!

So, you call for help and tear into the matrix of the system seeking to repair the plan and control the damage.

But, even though some may print, still you have lost a few pages in the process, so you put the book together anyway missing page 39 hoping they won't notice.

Our life is a book, you know, and we plan and plan, but when we feed the plan the provision; the end product doesn't match. But, Lord, we have planned so well!

We have hired the best experts in the field.

And, Lord, we have worked very hard…and now we are at 50 and we realize that we never got that degree; we didn't stay married to the man of our dreams; we never traveled on that vacation to the ski resort.

Now, Lord, we are too old to ski.

And, I think I'm missing pages 7, 16, and 39.

And, the presentation of my life to others looks patchy at best. I realize what happened, now that I have clear goals set in stone; Rock built on immovable desires of an eternal God who possesses all the power in Heaven and earth.

No one dares mess with His plan and who could compete with His provision?

Father, I trade in my plans for Yours, today. I lay them at the nail pierced feet of Jesus. Make me successful, dear Lord, in Your eyes. Complete my book the way it was intended to be written. Imprint me.

Print and Imprint

The difference between a print and an imprint is that a print impresses on and an imprint presses in. When we press into Him, He will impress upon us. Precious indentations of the Savior Divine into the heart.

He presses His points into your heart like sewing. He takes the diamond headed needle and mends our brokenness. He repairs our desires, threads His ribbons of love through the center of our being. And, if we can keep our eye on the needle, we threaded mind, soul, and body, through the place where we were meant to go.

We are threaded like a camel through His desires to His provision. Success.

Press

For when you press, you allow Me to imprint.
Like when a potato is carved out,
it leaves the imprint of the other side. You *reflect Me.*

Hands of Grace

Held in my hand, tucked in the plan
between the fingers tips of another.
Held by my Lord, not my brothers
Hands of grace forsake me not
Envelop, develop, and renew what's askew.
Fill my between places with your faces
sandwiched in the fingers of your graces.

Chapter 3

Spools of Wisdom

Too Much

And, do You revile me now, Lord because I have given too much? When You asked for a penny, I gave a dime.

When You asked for ten minutes, I gave twenty. I didn't have to. I wanted to.

Please understand, Father, that I gave because I wanted to. And, it hasn't cost me anything. How can I compare with what You have done for me? To stay up a night or two, what is that? To miss a few meals, what is that?

It is nothing compared to the pain You have had of knocking on the door of my heart day after day, year after year without response.

Certainly, Your knuckles are bruised and bloody from all that knocking. And, you, My Father, have stayed up night after night protecting me from the lion who creeps in the night.

Oh, without Your protection surely, he would have devoured me whole. Not to mention the strength You have provided to my very bones and flesh. For, day after day, You have energized me and revitalized my soul. To think that, for eternity past You have waited to find someone to share these messages with that bring water to a dry place.

These are messages of hope and love.

They enable You, for once to speak directly to Your Children. What an amazing thing! And, now You say I have given too much. I don't think so.

Given Too Much

The Dream:
It was supposed to be a break, but I never got any food and ended up returning late. I went too far from where I needed to return back in time. Somehow, I end up with a huge meat loaf and a small potato salad. There are problems as every turn. I can't find a table and then, there are issues with the silverware. But the time I get it all straightened out, my time is gone. I'm late.

So, I attempt to save some for myself and it doesn't work. The potato salad is really sliced eggs and the Tupperware won't close well enough to carry back with me. So, I give up and return to work, neglecting to eat at all. Along the way, I give everything away. It's just easier that way. But, I remain hungry.

Interpretation:
I have expended myself for others. My rest has overflowed to feed many. What was a little, grew to be a loaf. And, what I ordered was not what I received. I expended way more than I needed to, went much further out, and now I am finding it hard to get back on time. How could I possibly go that far in that amount of time and still get back to where I was supposed to be?

Even the stuff I thought was just for me ended up being finely sliced eggs. Ready to serve, what I received was what others needed to grow their vision, release their children and lead their own revolution. It was my meeting that I shared with them. My break became their mending point. For, when I took my break to Jesus, He repaired it and gave me much more than I needed.

And, still I haven't taken a break. And, my Father knows that I have expended myself for them. He knows how hungry I am, staring at the need for success, yet not having it. My hunger will only be satisfied when I see all of the books in print and realize that others are being freed to hear His voice for themselves through these writings. Until then, I will be hungry. My vision is unfulfilled, and my desire goes unmet because it is too big to meet at this time.

The problem is that my appetite has grown as my vision has grown. My vision has grown as He has directed me. At first I would have been happy to allow another to print my book. Then, my book turned into several. Then, He gave me the business, so I wasn't satisfied until it became stabilized. Now that it is stabilized, I am looking for the rest of the vision. He has rolled the vision out in front of me like a red carpet to board an airplane. I know that all must be in place before His total vision will take flight. And, I want to see it. I am hungry to see the fulfillment of the vision. I can't rest and will continue to be driven until I see it.

Understanding the heart of God has given me a burden for the lost. I know that minute by minute time passes and many are stamped with death and destruction. Of those that don't die, there are just as many that never hear the voice of God because they don't know how to tune their antenna to His. It's not that they don't want to, but they just know how. He wants to share how to hear His voice. Oh, as a Father, He has an urgent desire to share Himself with His Children in an intimate way. And, this drives me. Day and night, month after month, year after year. I will give my last breath for another because I know that by my writings many will be freed from the destruction of the world. Oh, to be used to shine a little thread of light into a dark place!

Threaded Through Training

Talk to me for just a bit, dear Lord. I know it's late but sleep can wait.

The unction of your function has been realized because in humility you came and in mercy you stayed. In service you were spent and your self you gave.

What you did was the true meaning of lent.

You sacrificed something for a specific time for a greater purpose. By faith you went.

But what makes today a major victory for us is that in the face of adversity you didn't flinch. You went to the river, focused on the other side and waited for Me to part the water. And, you knew when I did.

What you shared the way you shared it was so much more than anointing because of how you did it. You demonstrated it was the answer when you showed him where the gifts were supposed to leas one.

The interesting thing about today was that the battle I set up was one of your endurance and humility coupled with the surety with which you know you hear My voice. Physical endurance is easy because you have learned great discipline. Humility and servant heart have been taught. But in the open face of adversity you pushed through to bring about victory. Praise be to God! Sweet anointing of fire.

I went to a church and gave the Pastor the gift of interpretation of tongues anointing. There was adversity by an 'overseer' who thought I was and 'outsider' with trouble. But, I was humiliated in front of the congregation, waited all day, joined with the others to serve dinner, then at the right time, went up to the pastor and knelt down beside him sharing my heart. He responded positively and receive his anointing.

Draw Bridge of Faith

Take off your shoes. Exercise reverence in purity: Me to them.

Then, run the whole race; the whole truth; the whole area to presenting Me. It is like a colorful garment of provision brought to them. Draw the bridge. You see, it's not merely about My provision to you, but when you trust Me, you bring Mine to them. Because they are asking, I will come to their houses. The sail is complete. By your hands, the book is released. The fabric is built by your faith and obedience to My words.

Lower the bridge end to end. Extend your arms to Me. For, you my dear one, make the bridge by your hand brought through My provision threaded through the needle of your obedience. The eye is the obedience window.

And, will you stand there while the wind swirls? Let the tension build as the winds of potential destruction get closer and closer. Then, at just the right moment, I will swoop you up and lift you to the place of My intention.

Spool of Your Heart

But, Father, I left and I was not healed. The meeting is over. People file out. The singers are silent. Disappointment overwhelms my soul. Because what I hoped did not come about. One more time, my dreams have become shadowed by darkness. *But, child, that is not true. Are you God, that you know His mind? Are you the great physician that you can do surgery on your own heart? By what do you gage your wellness, my child? What you see? Your physical?*
That is an error.
For your flesh grows old with each breath.
This vigor is only for today. On your thinking?
Are you well because you see the scars removed,
the lump gone, the fractures set? Are you well
because you feel healed? Do we think our way
into the Kingdom of God? Do we feel our way
into His presence? No, my daughter. For
healing starts from the center of My
love and threads through My heart.
Like a spool of thread, I come up
through the center of your
being first, then start to
wind My threads of
wisdom, knowledge,
healing, and
deliverance
around.
You're not
full until you
are completely
wound up in Me.
When will that be, Lord?
Glory, My love. Glory.
But, you were wrong, you
know. Your healing starts as you
give the center and allow Me to thread My
ribbon of love through the spool of your heart.

Twisted too Tight

Easy becomes hard when we are twisted too tight. Like yarn
on a spool, it pulls at the threads. Sometimes we seem
to wind up in a different state wondering how we
got there and who we are.
God has provided
steps for us to help us.
He has given us His seven
Spirits to help us.
Wisdom, knowledge, Fear of the Lord,
Counsel, Might, Presence, and understanding.
He has provided a way to transfer those spirits.
to ours through giving us the Holy Spirit to
dwell with us We can become His
child as we call on Jesus to be
our
Savior.
We need to confess our sin
and keep a pure heart, seeking
His ways instead of ours.
We need
to be open to
rebuke. Others and His.
We need to be hungry for Him.
As we request His presence in our lives,
He will meet us at the place we are willing to go.
He loves us and wants us to be happy. He is our Father.

Crystal Clear Communion

The Dream:

At this church service they serve water for communion in crystal pitchers and stemmed water glasses. She says that it's the freshest water she has ever tasted. And, my dress is snagged because it starts to unravel as I walk out of the building. I try to stop it, but it starts again.

The color is coming off. Layer upon layer I am unraveling and taking off the threads of color. This service is one that provides for needs. They serve something that quenches our thirst for interaction with God and others. It's a beautiful serving in elegant containers; clean and sparkling, close to the sources of all: God.

It comes down from the rock, the stream of living water. As I walk from the building process, there is a snag. But, the snag only works to reveal my true colors. Even as I am snagged, I emit the colors I wear, and they are touched as I walk because as God is threading me through His provision I hand the information off to them. They are watching Him unravel my garment. Before their eyes, I am molting; I am revealing my true character underneath. I am a butterfly held in a cocoon that is about to be released. The silk is being unwound off my covering. Even as I reveal they are impressed at the purity of what I wear.

Interpretation:

As I begin to walk out from where my service is, I find that I get snagged. How I have enjoyed the fresh water of the words coming to me. And, what fun to put them into the wine glasses. It's the communion of the Holy Spirit shared with one another that is refreshing.

Now, the many colors of threads that I have gathered in the dreams and sat in the basket beside my chair are called to be used. He is unraveling my garment to use it for others. He is taking off the colors to weave other books.

Because I have left the threads, and not thrown them away, they are available for Him to use in books I never thought possible.

Twirled and Wrapped

The Dream:

As we have waited and hoped for the signs of the Holy Spirit many have doubted. And, indeed there are many of those even in our midst who doubt that the Holy Spirit lives for today. But, not this time. He comes as we are together each one calling out to Him individually to be filled. When He shows up the big guy doesn't fall like we assume He would; No He comes into our group face first. Oh, we have asked for the face of God to be revealed and now it is. This time He comes and lays us all out in a different way. Our organization has become His.

And, I have given you this dream just to give you a glimpse of what it looks like when I show up face first. I don't back into the room, silly. And, I don't come to you as a body, but individually, meeting you at your point of contact.

And let me show you where yours is:

I was lifted straight up off of the ground and brought down with a twirling motion. My body became as if it didn't exist in the physical sense. I found that I was wrapped in a powerful hand that twirled me and lifted me, setting me over others. I became alive to the Spirit and dull to the world.

Interpretation:

We are have been calling on the Holy Spirit to fill us and He is about to do it. In the dream His power is manifested to each person as he reaches toward Him. Each fall a different direction. For me, because of how I have sought Him, He comes to lift me straight up totally absorbed in the Spirit so that I become dull to the world and alive to Him. There is a twirling motion that He imparts to me. It is a twisting motion that happens as I wrap around Him and He wraps around me. He uses me to form a cord that is used for His purposes.

What He has done is wrap me around His finger like one would wrap a string in thought. I have become totally absorbed, intertwined, and enveloped by His Spirit. I am worsted like spun yarn from long fibers combed parallel and twisted hard. We have been spinning for some time going through hard things, so indeed, we are strong as we bind together. And, that cord is formed with the Scriptures, prophecy, faith and testimony.

Railroaded Gifts

The Dream:
We set up climate-controlled vehicles. All the rest fall in line like railroad cars behind the first.

The inside is not determined by the outside but rather the inside. It's a method of transporting the things of God which is controlled by the Holy Spirit and our ability to respond to Him once you understand how He directs your gifting.

The rest of the messages fall into place like cars on a track.

Temptation Obstructs Justice

Temptation obstructs justice because when Satan sneaks in and tempts you to show favor to yourself or others, then God's plans are obstructed. To smile for your own recognition or to sing for their favor obstructs God's plans.

Prophecy Threads

They couldn't figure out what the prophecy said, so they brought it to me. Even then I had to ask God for the answers. I waited for them, then I waited for Him and I waited for the right time to share with them. *Prophecy is a three handed pull when you only have two. That is because you need the hand of God to pull you through.*

Fluffy Prayer

Fluffy prayer is what I do best. Recite the need and follow the rest.
Certainly, God knows my heart, need I say it to Him?
If He knows all, then I can skim.
So, I recite my prayer, learned long ago
and hope it will work; that my path will show.

Certainly, the one who penned this was spiritual to the core
It is certainly full of lore.
But, still, I wonder: is this all God wants?
Recite my prayer at my lunch,
then chow down the fries and eat my brunch.

Or does He want more? This I dread.
For, what would I say, certainly I can't come up with words? How do I voice my desires out loud, so they don't sound absurd? I would rather us a prayer I have learned,
one that I know will work
And, know for surety, that He won't call me a jerk.

But, I am just not sure, any more,
perhaps I need to change my core.
Maybe He wants for us, perhaps what we desire. And maybe our desire, with an open heart is our part Are we not meant to grab another's prayer
and put it as our own
When we have need for conversation on the prayer phone.

It could be what He wants is what we have got
an open line to our soul, the same one that we have sought.
An open heart, an honest view, a window to our soul,
Perhaps what He desires, can actually make us whole.
What if the prayer we prayed became a prayer that stayed?
What of that?
What if truth be known our barren heart was shown
From stem to stern and back?
What then?

Double the dose, power repose
to free a bird that was kept in jail.
To open our soul to the one who loves us true,
The one who died to lead the truth to me and to you.

Free bird fly to the lips of my mouth.
Sail through the air. Fly, fly, fly south.
Bring the truth of my heart to the Lord Divine
Reveal my desire, echo over the line.
Cross to Your cross, take my learned prayer and mend.
Tack some truth on the hem and give it a fresh bend.

Bring it to Your court, embrace it with Your desire.
Show me of Your fulfillment and teach me of Your fire.

Recite Your love to me and I will return
The voice of fulfillment that is Your concern.
Renew my request and grant me words that will become true
Eloquently matched by a God who is in love with me and you.

Pushed by a Hand

   Pushed by a hand, I cannot feel. Molded by fingers, I do not see.
Held within his grasp, I live. Waiting to see what He will make of my life.

The Cabinet of Your Heart

When was the last time you opened the cabinet of your heart?

Is it a place you have forgotten all about, or is it a place you frequent daily?

When was the last time you opened the cabinet of your heart?

Are you afraid of what you will find there?

What if you took everything out of that cabinet and laid it all on the counter?

Then, what if you determined to sort it all out: throw the trash away, recycle that which you have duplicates of and share the rest?

Are you brave enough to open the cabinet of your heart and set all those things in front of God, then ask Him about what should be put back in there?

Sometimes we need spring cleaning.

Other times, we need to give all that old stuff away, fill the trash with the rest and leave the doors open.

Help us to be brave enough, Dear Father to open the door to the cabinet of our heart.

Envision the Revision

God is next to what He plants. A problem is that we have a hard time envisioning the revision because we fall in love with our own work and don't want to change it. We forget that this is a river and not a lake. We need to get into the flow.

Keel of Direction

The Dream:
A word of change is sent down from the captain's office. He gives the signal to those entrusted with changing the direction of the keel. There is a turning of the keel, and a churning of the water. There is a rumble and a momentary backwash as currents meet. The current that was set up as the ship propelled forward ceases and a change ensues. The current that was generated by the rotation of the propeller meets its new current. The moving water meets itself, causing a mighty rumble. The forward motion caused by the propulsion of the water out the back of the ship ceases. It has to in order to enable the ship to turn. But, it doesn't stop all together, for it is necessary to keep water moving over the propeller to enable direction.

When the keel is turned, the ship eases to the right at the word of the captain. Does He control the ship? No, his word controls the ship. What controls the ship is the movement of the keel and the direction that the water pours over the propeller.

There doesn't even need to be a propeller if there is wind and a sail.

That is the difference between dreams and hearing the voice of God in the daytime?

When you hear the voice at night, it is like driving a motorized ship. He declares the words, then, you follow them. The only thing needed is the power of the Holy Spirit to bring about their forward movement. There is a rumbling in your bowels and a shaking as you do what He has instructed. But, you have no responsibility because you have merely done what the captain has asked.

When you hear the voice of the captain in the daytime, it's different.

He is not on the ship. He's the whisper in the wind of your soul. Do you hear the whisper?

You cannot see wind, so you cannot see His word. But, will you move the keel to the words?

Because, this ship is no different than the other; it turns with the keel that is in your hand. There is a false safety with the mechanics of the motorized ship that when we pull certain levers and push specific buttons, the keel will turn. But, we can't see it from where we stand, we expect it to work as we desire. What of mechanical failure?

But, the galleon is awesome. Catch the winds and move across the sea at amazing speed with only the help of the sail. Oh that we could learn how to put up our sail. For, when we extend our soul to Him, He will fill it with air. His winds of truth blow against our soul when it is extended to Him. But, still, we must remember that He has put the keel into our hand. It is our life. We can still buck against the wind. We can tack.

So, even though we have learned how to extend our soul to Him and catch His words, if we don't do what He says, then the ship won't go in the right direction. We will be buffeted and tossed, put into a position where we must toss our provisions overboard in order to survive. We will find ourselves dreading life and looking for dangerous undercurrents, reefs and rocks. Our desire for joy departs and we will abort the cruise. The pleasure cruise turns nightmare, and our dreams are bound to sink below the surface of the provision of them. Have we boarded a sinking dream, or simply forgotten to take note of the winds?

Did we send ourselves on our own mission, or did we stop listening to His directions? Where is mercy when we need it? Just over the horizon of His love. Ask and He will send His ship meant to bring mercy to His drowning children, drifting out of control buffeting His directions.

Is it our fault that we have not listened? Probably. But, remember, He calls us His children, so we can always call on the love of a Father set against His child to give us an island when we need one.

Faith as a Mustard Seed

At what point did we decide that dreams are more reliable than listening to God in the daytime?

It is a problem with trust. Faith is the assurance of things not seen. If you need to see something to believe it, then when I come at night and show it to you, it causes the faith to be grown. Dreams are like seeds. Sometimes I give a seedling, like going to the nursery and buying a plant that is already growing. It doesn't take much faith to grow tomatoes from a plant that already has tomatoes on it, does it?

Dreams are like that. When I give a dream, it is like a plant. They are given at all levels of growth. Sometimes, I give a plant that is already nearly full size. When I give a plant that is nearly mature, it is easy to see what I expect. You simply need to look at the leaves and fruit to figure out what kind of a plant it is, then, plant it in your life.

So, when I give a dream that is already grown, it is easy to understand, and they believe it. I show them a picture and correlate it for them. When I put the actual situation in the dream and speak the truth clearly, then, they have no problem with it.

And, sometimes, if the message is important, I give it several times, clearly. It doesn't take much faith.

But, think about it this way: suppose you purchase the tomato plants before they have blooms? Do you trust your ability to plant them in good soil and tend them enabling them to grow up and produce? Will your eyes be alert to their needs? What if they get aphids or the sun is too bright? Do you know how to run off the enemies and shield them from disaster?

But, to take a seed is a different story. Are you willing to wait for it to grow? Are you confident enough to be able to choose soil and know when to water? Do you know which window to put the tender plant in? When I said that faith was like a mustard seed, what do you think I meant? A seed is meant to be grown.

Faith is alive when you take some small word from Me and allow it to be planted in your heart. It is all about the small words. It's not about the big, elegant dreams: It's easy to believe them, but, who would dare to believe a small vision into the screen of her mind?

What happened is that you followed the vision. It wasn't the dream, but the vision that carried you through. And, it will continue to carry you because, remember the story, the birds are able to nest in the tree grown from the mustard seed?

Owning Kingdoms

Is it our fault that we have not listened? Probably. But, remember, He calls us His children, so we can always call on the love of the Father which is set toward His child to give us an island when we need one.

Power Reach

What delight exists beyond what you can touch. Reach out. Stretch your hand as far as it can go. Then bridge the distance to Me, by faith.

It is like electricity. You can just get close and reach out. Let the tension build in anticipation. For, I have reached as far as I can. I am Spirit, remember? But, there still is a gap. Like a park plug, you can tighten the gap by increasing the spark. Fire of the Holy Spirit combined with desire, increases the faith gap…which actually decreases the distance between us.

Threads of Hope

Threads of hope, threads of light,
Threads of love, envelop me bright.
Threads of joy, thread my soul
Between your fingers, make me whole.
Wholly Yours, wholly theirs
Between, in and through
Wholly threaded, guided, and pushed.
Threads of hope, let me be
guided by Your hand, from You to me.
To them, that they may see
the You, not the me, the way it's supposed to be.
Your light, Your sight, Your might.
Your threads of love, threads of hope,
twisted colorful, fibers of rope.
Attached to a ring of eternal set,
goals intertwined, meshed, once met.
Between you and Me, Me and you
Them and us, me in Thee.

Mercy Caps

Caps at both ends: grace and mercy. Be threaded.

Unity with God can only be achieved His way. He is the one in charge, not us. The Word doesn't say, "pull on Me, and I will come to you."

Yet, you attempt to grab onto His garment to keep Him nearby. A real father cannot be steered by grabbing onto his shirt, yet we think we can steer God by grabbing onto His righteousness. If we cling to His righteous garment, then, it does not mean that He will stay.

Like a real father, He has purposes of His own. Like a real father, He cannot allow His children to dictate His purposes because they cannot see with His eyes. Remember, He calls us children because we have characteristics like them. Our eyesight is limited by our level; how tall we are. Like children, we will never be at His level unless He personally reaches out His arms and picks us up. He is the one that raises us to His level. Then, we can see around.

But, do we see from His vantage? Does a child see from His father's vantage if he is put on his shoulders? Nearly, but he never loses those immature eyes. He looks for things of his own interest, not those of the interest of his father. Only when his father points out things, does he strive to focus in that direction.

We are children. When God lifts us up; He raises us from our lowly position and shoulders us, we will have opportunity to see things from His viewpoint. But, let us not forget we are still children. Although, we may be in a position where we could see all that He sees, we won't because it's just no our desire. Our own needs and desires will always continue to drive our vision.

Pass the Shuttle

We are woven like on a loom.
He moves us one way, then passes the shuttle.
Then He moves us another way, then passes it again.
I can feel Him within. He doesn't constrict or restrict.
But He rewrites the main points
then threads us
through
the
middle of them.
He changes our desires.
This is my desire to honor you from the inside out
You become shown to others as you are on My Inside
Then, we learn to become transparent to others.
Then they see Christ in us, the hope of glory.

Chapter 4

Woven Promises

Weaving the Picture

Notice that the bridge gets smaller toward the center as it stretches to span the distance of the ravine. As my hand reaches toward God, He will reach toward me. It is where His hand touches mine that we form a bridge of understanding for others to walk across. This bridge is one of sharing the ability to understand His voice.

As I have reached up, now I will reach out. And, as I truly believe that I am reaching out to them in the face of Him, I am reaching out to Him again. So, again, there will be a miracle of Him touching me. As He has touched me with insight to see His voice for myself, so, He will touch me in the face of them. The difference is that when I touch them, they will receive His touch for it is His power that flows through me to them. Again, it is a threading. As I am threaded by His hand through the provision toward the need, He will push me into His fabric. I will become the tapestry for others to look at.

And isn't a needle sharper toward the end?

Yes, Lord. So, you are sharper now. For I am not pushing the blunt end through the fabric. I have threaded you through the needle, now I will sew up the plan, bind the stitch and mend a situation that needed to be repaired long ago.

I will seek to mend broken ties; broken hearts; broken lives with my words as they learn to listen to my voice. You, my love are a diamond headed needle that I am pushing through the fabric to stitch a colorful picture of my love for my children. You are a picture made beautiful by My hand. Picture perfected by Me. For, you have had touch ups by the master artist, here in my studio. And, the tip can be lonely, but they will follow. Just don't look back. There is a picture to weave. We have only just begun. {Written April 25th, 2005}

Pitiful Faith

If we have been found to believe in a God that fails to bring us to the end of His promise, then we are most to be pitied. It's night without sunrise; a pregnancy without a birth; a broken dream. We must ask God for the faith to believe that He not only gives promises but fulfills them.

Tangled Threads of Hope

And, you are discouraged because you looked on line and didn't find your name. And, you are discouraged because there weren't hundreds of sales today.

And, you are discouraged because the advertisement doesn't go out until next week. And, you are discouraged because you compared yourself with others. Did you find your reflection there?

No, my Lord, I didn't.

Am I suddenly a liar because you are not satisfied by your search?

Are you the eyes of the body? Do you know what I am doing at the other end of things? Just because you can't see what is going on doesn't mean that nothing is going on. And, did you find your reflection there?

No, my Lord, I didn't.

Why didn't you find your reflection there?

I didn't find my reflection there because that is not to be my mirror. I am not supposed to be reflecting myself on others.

But, what I was looking for was someone just like me doing the same thing.

No you weren't. You wanted to see that I had made your site at the top. It hasn't happened there yet. Believe me, in my mind it has.

But, Father, I am afraid that I will run out of resources before it gets there. At what point do you trade those promises in for real stuff? The whole ship is going to go upside down any minute if there isn't provision here.

It won't go up side down. It's just a tip. A settling to make sure that it won't. Others need time to iron out a few other things with the Web site. It needs to be user friendly from the other side. And, they nearly got it. It's more about their goals becoming ours. They had their own goals in mind, now they are seeing the extent of becoming part of the vision. They hadn't invested much until now. Let them settle into the vision. Let them have an opportunity to pray it into being.

But, Father, I am starting to look like a liar. How can I bare to lay them off those I have hired? It makes all of the things that I have written invalid if You don't pull me through.

At the right time, I will bring you through. Why would I not thread you through? Do you think I am playing a game with you. Do I tempt you to run you over? Am I a Father who hates you? Listen to Me. I love you and don't want to hurt you. You need to be patient. I will bring you through, but there are many others that also need to come.

If I don't have income soon I will owe the printer and the tax people and my husband will be mad at me. I don't like this box that you have put me into. And, what happened to my prayer partner who I thought would be by my side in faith believing in the promises with me?

What happened to your friend? He quit on his own. It's easy to be on the winning team, but when you are marching into a battle, out numbered, you need those that are sturdy and convinced of the victory in the battle. If he is not sturdy, then surely he will run at the face of the enemy. Why should those who are not willing to pay the price reap the rewards?

I am sorry, Lord. I love you. Forgive me for being unfaithful. I have wandered off on a trail that wasn't my own. It seems that every time I wander off, I pay. I lay my burden at your feet. I guess this is too big for me to carry. Please take it off my shoulders, one more time.

Cap-Sized Ship

I stood there on the bow of this mighty sailing vessel as it sailed through the harbor. What a magnificent vessel God had given to me: to be understand His voice through dreams, visions and quiet contemplation in prayer. So, I stood tall waving the flag He had put into my hand trying to attract attention to His purposes.

But, the problem was that, even though I stood on the bow of a mighty sailing vessel, others weren't impressed because it seemed as though the ship was upside-down. And, they declared me a crazy woman. For who would stand on the bow of a ship which was capsized and wave a flag except that she wanted to be rescued by another.

So they came to rescue me. Some brought grand business ideas, while others brought high interest loans. Some determined that I must be bored and need a ministry, so they invited me to join 'their boat'.

Oh, but I declared, "Why would I want to jump ship when I have been given such a wonderful vessel that moves on its own power?"

"Yes," They comforted me, "But there is no control with your vessel. There is no one at the helm, so what will keep you from running aground?"

Indeed, this ship does not run by man-made power, but the power of God. And it is faith which supplies the ability to see the map to know where it will go. So, there is power and direction; it's just that women don't normally stand on a ship which is capsized and wave a flag.

But, I did. Because I believed it was true and I was willing to stand on the promises. And, I knew I was standing on a ship which was turned upside-down. They assumed I wasn't aware of what I was doing. They are wrong. But, what they didn't factor into the equation was the power of God to turn the ship right side up any time He wanted.

And, He did. January 17th 2007 God breathed life into the dream and flipped the ship over. It was an easy thing for a God with such big hands. All of a sudden, the huge foundation which I had been laying for four years came to life. God raised walls of the building. All this time we had been laying foundation underground. Indeed I looked like a crazy woman because just as I would finish foundation in one area, He would send to me to another. And, who spends four years just building foundation? Someone who is planning on building a large structure. So, on January 17th 2007 He turned my accounts. All of a sudden the woman who owed $100,000 didn't. All of a sudden, books sprung up, one after another. The knowledge level had peaked. I now knew computer programs {InDesign, Acrobat, Avery, Photoshop, Illustrator, Dreamweaver, Cubase} so I didn't need to ask anyone for answers because I already had them. And, when He rose the walls of this enormous structure it was as if a huge sailing vessel was up righted. Wonderful billowing masts fly into the wind. Beautiful carved decks with mahogany railings line the sun deck.

And, after extensive training, He sent me to the helm and gave me the wheel. Now I direct Glory Bound Books Ltd. God has set up everything so that if someone has a manuscript and hands it to me, I can edit, format, print, bind and register the copyright within the same day. In the time it takes him to go pick up our lunch, I can produce a book. When he returns from picking up the lunch, I could hand him his finished book. And, I have all of the components for a sound studio production of the books. In fact we are just finishing our first animated reading of a children's book 'Sharing Ole Lumpy'.

Last week I had four pieces of printing equipment delivered. God gave me $8000 to spend on equipment, but when I prayed, I got everything I needed for $4000. So, now I still have $4000. And, the translations abound. Ole Lumpy will come out in Korean. I have two other children's books in foreign languages: One in Jordanian, and one in Tai. All of the Pantuffle books will be translated into German as soon as I can get the CD into the mail. We will begin the Creative Arts Explosion Nights in two cities next month. Karna and I will go back and forth to share in her town and mine. This is a program of helping artists, musicians and writers to learn how to publish their works.

Next week I will obtain the licenses for Music Publication so that we can release many songs. You see there are three areas to Glory Bound Books Ltd. There are Books, Children's books and sound. So, you might say that this ship has three masts.

And, they don't laugh at me anymore because I stand on the bow of mighty ship with the masts billowing in the wind. Yet the question remains: Was this ship less of a ship before it was turned right side up? Remember: God's missions come by faith through grace, and that not of yourself: it is a gift of God, not as a result of works that we cannot boast in using our own strength to build His structure.

Fly to His Aspirations

Dream:

We all started out on this transport together, but everybody else got off except my sister and me. I am left in the back serving. And the jet seemed to change into a more compact, faster jet. We take off the runway and the ride is really unstable. The pilots in the cockpit look like professionals, but I am worried because I still have my cups to drink. So, I decide to down them rapidly. I'm not buckled into a seat because I am working so hard.

And, just as the plane leaves the runway, it makes a hard bank. I keep thinking I should really find a seat and get secured into a place, but the speed is too fast and I have no time.

And, in the midst of this hard banking and instability, Karna asks me to brew a cup of hot chocolate. And, I actually contemplate trying to do this in a jet taking off from an airport going around 300 miles an hour at a severe bank. My problem is that I have all I can do to stabilize the cups on my own table, let along manage to serve her.

I scream to the pilots, "Are we going to crash?"

And, they respond, "No, we are not going to crash. This is the way." When I look out the front window, we are heading down a wide road leaving the city. There are just a couple of intersections with green lights in them. Then, we will follow the freeway and fly around a couple of rock spires {like Sedona, Arizona.} And, we will never land again.. we will simply go around a couple of big aspirations and level out our wings.

Interpretation:

As we are moved into 'taking off' from the runway in the transport which God has given us, it may cost something. The band refers to money, sleep, time, or anything else which we have and must 'expend' to make God's vision come to pass. Sometimes we are 'spent' yet others come to us and ask for more.

The dream provides a humorous picture of how we attempt to serve sometimes. We may be working very hard to get the ministry which God has entrusted to us 'off the ground', yet in the midst of it all, try to fit into our schedule someone else' s desire. A cup of hot chocolate is hardly a true need, yet because I am in a position where I could provide it, I try to fit it into my schedule. Notice that my sister is buckled securely into her seat and asks me to wait on her. We may be spending and spending our own money to put a 'show into place', yet others don't realize it and hold out their hand to us as well. We may become tempted to become irritated at their behavior, but we must remember that, if we have truly given to the ministry which God has entrusted to us, then we probably haven't told others how hard we are 'banked', so they have no idea how much further they are compromising our position when they ask us to serve.

I believe the end of the dream demonstrates that when we take off the ground, like putting the key into the keyhole, and opening the door, sometimes, the way isn't completely clear. Perhaps, there are a few boxes that need to be pushed aside to get through the door. In the dream we flew through a couple of intersections {we move through a few sections} and then fly around spires {fly to the aspirations}.

Note that the interpretation of this dream is in the words and the pictures provide the humor.

Kapeseus Antemeus: Responsive Prayer

This buttonhole fastening is a huge task. Take the things you are given to pray them in. It is like sewing on a button, and then pushing the button through the buttonhole.

Kapeseus Antemeus

This word means to be threaded and pushed, continually held within the hand of your maker from one place to the next.

For, it is by your own prayer and His answer that the whole process happens. I am pushed through to the 'whole' when I am tacked onto where I belong and threaded through an opening to close a gap in His garment of complete Salvation.

Canopy

A covering to protect you from in climate weather.
Shade in the bright sun, and finding dryness amidst
the rain.
A fabric rises to be between us and the things
we have no control over, but would bring us
discomfort. We are saved from sunburn
and drenching. The fabric of our belief
covers everything we do. It is a banner
raised over our head. Faith in that
belief is what
protects us from
weather elements.
For, when we believe
in the only true God
and we trust in that
belief, we uphold
Him in faith.
It does
not matter the weather.
He stands over us whether or
not whatever happens, through
all. He is our shield in the weather.

A Matter of Weaving

It is a matter of weaving the right fabric using the fruits of the Holy Spirit, the gifts of the Holy Spirit and insight into the dark mysteries of God which allow the release of a mighty flow of this spiritual movement. It's a combination that opens a door of understanding the voice of God through dreams and quiet contemplation in prayer.

Just like weaving fabric you must take the threads one by one and weave them to form a complete picture that others can see. At first when you began to gather fibers of understanding, you didn't even know they were for a tapestry. There was information given at the time on the steps that were needed. Because each step was large, new and intense, I needed you to focus completely on it apart from the others. Not until I had several steps or threads could I begin to show you how they wove into a complete picture.

When you make fabric, it's not a solid piece with fruit drawn on it, but interwoven colors of threads displayed at specific times along the way. First you have the colors, and then you must learn how to weave them together. After you have the threads, learning to weave is easy. It's the gathering of the threads that is difficult. And, once you know where to get them, you will have a steady supply of them.

So, opening the flow of the release of the Holy Spirit into the daily lives of people is very complex. And, it's like writing a book; it must be done by one person that can concentrate on the project long enough to work on the fabric from start to finish. Once you have the threads and weave the fabric, rolling it off is easy. For you, the threads of understanding were gathered one by one in the desert and through the long hours in your study at the computer with your Bible on the table. You had to overcome sinfulness, depravity, laziness, pride, and a mix mosh of things which were enemies. Anything you hold on to is your enemy because when your hands are not empty, I can't put into them what needs to be there.

I love you, because you linger. When I taught you how to empty your hands, you lingered for a while; several months. So, I showed you how to free up from old oppressions. It was like after dinner conversation. We had done all that needed to be done for the day, but, because you enjoyed my company so much, I continued to speak. And, it was natural to continue along the same subject line.

And, the fabric became woven when you realized that they could become books. See, each book is like a design in the fabric that displays another aspect of learning in prayer. What we have here is prayer cloth. Then the books are displayed together in a design on the fabric. And, when the fabric is finished, you simply roll it out. It becomes usable to others.

You see, this movement of releasing the gifts of the Holy Spirit has to be all at once. I don't release a few fruits at once because they all are imprinted in the fabric of dreams. That's the movement; the flow; the direction of today. You don't unravel, you roll it out. Not as individual pieces, but visual of the whole together. That is why I have continually instructed you to tell them of books that are not finished. These aren't stair steps, but steppingstones all on the same level.

When laid out, they form a mosaic. Only when someone stands back and focuses on it, can they see it.

In order for you to lay the stones, I had to give them to you, one by one. This mosaic was so large, that it took a while. And, the problem with this project is the power level. It's like learning to work with something extremely dangerous. The voltages of power are like lightening, so you were continually at risk of being destroyed if you touched it the wrong way. Also, like a science marvel, of new discovery, you were constantly at risk of the enemy stealing your ideas and burning off his own copy. You had to keep them hot enough so he couldn't touch them. That involved speed. It was a fast project. It was fast weaving of the fabric to open the doors to dreams. Welcome. And congratulations.

The fabric is done. It needs to be totally completed, but at least you can show them the design. And, now you are ready to roll it off the plant. What we have made is a hybrid fruit tree. By grafting several types of fruits on the same tree, I am displaying fruit for all seasons. Amazing. January 15, 2006

{This message refers to the Twelve Steps in the Garden which are ten books that I have been working to thread all of these principles through. You can find the list in the back of this book or on line at www.gloryboundpublishing.com.}

Pop Beads

Beads of understanding threaded on His love Brought by His grace and mercy to adorn us. One by one we can see how they attach.

Then, we attach the colors to form a necklace. To one a necklace to another a yoke. It's the same. The means by which the Kingdom of God Is carried through our field. We pull the cart which contains all that is needed. We pull the plow, we pull the crops, we pull the seeds.

Coordinated Flow

When Mom wisdom sees that I might be in danger, she shoos me out of that place. There are enemies lurking in the Churches. They were heads without purpose because they have no connection to the body. It has been dismembered by those claiming authority, pulling for power intent on mimicking God. They lord over you.

What you need in the family of God is more like two sisters teaching one another to ice skate. You need to work on flow and coordination. The big sister teaches the younger to ice skate by holding her hand tight while she spins and twirls with timing and coordination. There is precision within their movements which allow them to display the beauty keeping their balance. Her sure-footedness keeps her sister in line until she can learn for herself to be kept in line with her own feet surely planted on the ice.

Anointing Sprinkles

To share anointing is like sprinkles on a cupcake.
It makes yours to have more colors.
It add diversification to your message.

Fabric of Say

Thank you, Father for Your love,
Thank You Father, above
Amazing grace has touched my face
The face of a child with love
Thank you, Father, what can I
say How can I tell others to pray
The way You have shown how they haven't known
Thanks to their Father has grown

And they'll thank Me for you, yes it's true
Because by effort the fabric has come
A weaving of love, and grace from above
Shown to you, and then some.
Your cup was filled then continued to flow
Arms outstretched you continued to show
Grace and mercy to Me your God
Your Father, Your mother, your brother, your rod

By the lightening rod that you held in your hand
And stretched to the sky, I have brought mending to the land
You have become the one bringing the flow on in
Grounding the light, relenting the sin
Calling to purity and holiness within.
Holding out your hands to Me leaving your feet on earth.
Heaven has touched down. I have given birth
To plans that were never know. I have clearly shown
That I love, I live, above I give without coming down.

Because I don't need to bend the light to suit your ways
Only show where to put your hands to collect my says.
Gather my thoughts arrange them in order
To weave the fabric, decorate the border
And make my love shown day after day
As I enter your world with my say.

Gift Extension

Power
Miracles
Anointing
Repentance

All these they receive when you go back because that is how these gifts are extended. The extension of My hand is through mercy, but you need to walk into it. They are like clothes hanging on a clothesline; you have to walk into them. Walk into the adornment where I put you. It is a combined effort to walk in the Spirit.

Help on the Other Side

The dream:
And, we end up on the other side of where they wanted to go. So I took them to the mall. My daughter wanted to shop, so she asked me for money. Of course, I will give it to her because she is my daughter. And, we look over the shelves. There is really not much for her to buy. But, when she finds something, I'll help out.

Interpretation:
God has brought me to the other side of where I wanted to go. Now, he has brought me to the mall. At this time there isn't much to spend money on, but when I need it, He will provide. I'm His daughter.

Coming over the Ridge

The Dream:

We were on a long walk to the sea. My husband and I came to a cliff and I got scared. Others were going down by hanging onto the pink flowering fruit trees, but I was unsure. I looked for an easier way. The ground was slippery with loose rocks and sand. We could see where we wanted to go but were frustrated at how to get there. My fear of falling all the way down the cliff made us walk along the ridge for a while.

Then, I figured it out and when I did it was OK. I used the fruit trees and it was a graceful climb down to the sea.

Interpretation:

Jesus, as my husband, has been with me every step of the way. He has instructed me through the use of the gifts of the Holy Spirit using the fruits the Spirit. But, the way was steep and the bank was intensive. I went through a lot of money and became frightened at the numbers.

I was worried that I would fall completely in debt without hope of recovery, so I stopped. I walked along the ridge for a while. I found that I couldn't stay there, however, because even the ridge was unsafe. The footing was slippery, at best. And, I kept looking to where God had set my heart; His goals, and I wanted to get there. I just couldn't work through the banking system to get there. I thought it was the finances that were impeded, but, in reality, it was my inability to work through the gifts that He had entrusted to me and trust Him at His Word that stalled me.

My own fear kept me from the goals of going where I knew I was supposed to be. It is by His grace using the gifts of the Holy Spirit that He has enabled me to work down the bank to the celebration.

He has helped to bring me to the place of seeing. What I have seen has become a dream to reality.

At the sea we found a celebration in progress. There were booths all set up waiting for us. My husband gave me a container that was empty, and I took it to another booth and filled it. But, when he came back to me, He pointed out that I had only filled that container halfway. It actually held twice as much as I thought it did.

And, we lost the others who started out with our party. But, that's OK. They weren't ready.

When I reached the place where the business was built, I saw that everything was ready for operation. I found myself in the middle of a celebration. People are celebrating the fact that dreams can be understood. They are celebrating that God is speaking and someone can understand giving them the ability to understand, as well.

And, Jesus gave me my empty container. I took it to a place where I thought I had all I could handle, and when He came back, He told me that I could actually handle twice as much. Bigger numbers, more books, more titles, more stuff. He said that I could actually handle twice as much volume as I thought I could. I guess I have arrived at the place I need to be. It's just a matter of asking Him to fill the rest of the space within my heart with His goals. Amen.

Seam Ripper

If you can figure out how something is sewn together, then you can take it apart at the seams. The enemy has stuff He has built.

Ask God to show you how it's put together, then, just take a seam ripper to it.

Truth in our hand is what rips apart all that is not of God. There are things that seam OK but aren't.

Check the seams at the seams, then, tear apart what isn't built properly. For, who needs a shirt with three arms, or a pair of pants with one leg? The Devil builds his garments with his instructions, and they are not fit for us to walk in.

God of Comfort

God of comfort, God of love
In thee I take refuge, in the wings of the Dove.
God of comfort, God of love
To you I give my heart. Take it with you to above.
God of comfort, God of love
My heart, I lend, I give it a shove.
God of comfort, Spirit of Truth
Rest my heart, build a booth.
Wonder of life, image of Peace
Grant unto my heart grace with a new lease.
In thee do I cope, I give You the rope.
God of comfort, Spirit of grace
Ever present Father, let me see Your face.
Here is my hand, my eyes, my voice.
I give You my life, come let us rejoice.
For the God of comfort, the Spirit of love
has brought to me His gift from above.
A lure that will entice, love that will remain
Love everlasting, love that will sustain.

Boxed Options

It seems like no matter what the question is, the answer is to ask God.

They gave us a dream. We only know how to pursue it our way until we ask Him something different. Thinking we were in a bad spot and in a jam, I came along and asked. It doesn't make sense to pursue other options first when they will surely fail. He has already given us the best.

The real problem is that we pursue what we think in the best instead of asking and getting it. We are pent up; boxed in our options.

And, just because we have company in our box, doesn't make it right. Others are simply boxed with us. It merely means that there is a bunch of us who don't want to ask. So, it's a matter of our will.

Another matter is that we want to be right and are afraid we will be wrong. So, we make do. Sounds like pride. So, I think I will take my chances and ask Him for the best answer.

Then, even though it may take a while because it comes in the mail, then, at least the answer is not questionable when it comes. Not almost, but for sure. Even though we want the answer, we often ask everyone around us and stumble around with fragments of Scripture to do what we hope is the best. Yet the answer is at our fingertips we need to ask, then, learn how to listen for the answer. The answer doesn't do any good if we can't interpret it. It's a foreign language until we sort it out.

Walking on my Hands

At 47 I finally learned to walk on my hands.

What I realized was that the Christian walk is a balancing act. What we do is the basis for how we move.

And, it's by faith. For certainly, @ 47 years old, I can't think to walk on my hands without help to stay up there. *The bill has come due and my daughter must pay, but it's been paid for already. She only needs to accept the provision for the payment.*

Colorful Threads of God

Compost is made of old food thrown out piled up
provides fertilizer for new growth. Put the
fragments in a pile.
If they never seem to add up, at least
they will provide a basis for new growth.
Sometimes, when God speaks, we don't quite get it.
We reach out and only grasp a few golden threads.
But, not enough to weave a picture. Just put
the threads in a bag, next to your easy
chair. Who knows, you may be working
a project and find a color you need?
And, like an artist, I favor certain
colors.
Blue is one of My
favorites. And green,
and brown. A
message is conveyed
in the intensity
of the hues,
the tones.
The
Brighter
ones
are reserved,
like chairs reserved in a
restaurant, for special people.
They are reserved for
My special guests. So, when you find someone
in love with Me, who is also colorful, give him special
honor, For he sits at My reserved table, in the banquet of My love.

Chapter 5

Tapestry of Faith

Honoring Grand Father

The Dream:
We went to grandpa's funeral, but my daughter and I got bored and left before the ceremony. We returned and my shoe broke right before we went through the entrance. I met my sister leaving as we were returning. I guess we missed the middle. I suppose they missed me, but they didn't provide a place for me.

At first, I thought I might be a support to others, but this huge screen was in the way of my vision. When it got in my uncle's way, he moved it because he was in charge. So, even though my shoe broke, and the style was wrong, I went back and wore them anyway. I found the desserts too sweet. Who needs pumpkin everything? It is the wrong season. And, amidst it all they pointed out that there was something of mine which I had left. Obviously, I was important to grandpa.

What good does it do to go to a funeral and miss the main point: to honor and pay tribute to the one who has passed on? It makes you wonder who they honored because there were so many things in the way.

Interpretation:

Our intention was to honor our grand Father, but we neglected to wait for direction and left. Then when we returned to honor Him, I realized that what I had assumed was true, wasn't true at all. But, I patched up as best I could and returned to honor him.

I met my sister coming and going. They didn't make a place for me and at first, I thought I might be a support to someone else. But the big screen that God had put in my way, blocked my vision to see others. When God's vision got in his way, he pushed it aside because he declared that he was in charge.

With my brokenness and out of style for today, I went back to honoring the father anyway because I knew it was right. And, I brought the Church with me. {My daughter.} And, what they missed was what I had to offer; I knew Him and he knew me. so, I had something to say. It sounds like testimony of a relationship with a grand Father.

Interpretation note: If you are trying to learn how to interpret your own dreams, this is a good example of a 'tight' dream interpretation. You can take the words which I used in the interpretation and see how they run parallel to the dream. What I have done is 'discard' the pictures and take the words. The book FireFly, which is the next book in the 12 Steps in the Garden, explains how to get the words from your dreams. The sub-title of that book is: dreams aren't meant to be silent movies: they have words. You can order it from Amazon or directly from our office.

My God Grew Yesterday

How big do you think God is?
Mine grew yesterday.
When I spent the day with someone else.

My God grew yesterday.
Taller, wider, and deeper than deep,
My God grew yesterday in ways never thought possible
My go grew yesterday.

When she told me of pain, anger, desperation, and loneliness
My God grew yesterday.
When she told me of abandonment, misery, grief, remorse
My God grew yesterday.

And, I saw the signs, I really should have known That my image of Him would grow
When I found the God seeing books, the tarot cards, and the demonstration of intimacy with nature on the sills of the 60-year-old house. Surrounded by clam shells lining the walkways amid rose bushes and cement garden animals.
I really should have taken my clue. My God was going to get bigger.
I really should have known.

My God grew yesterday
I really should have known
Amid dusty throw rugs and plastic flowers dimmed by sunlight of days gone by.
My God grew yesterday.
For the life she lived has now grown dim. At least that's what they said. But, let me tell you friend, they were wrong, I know that for sure because My God grew yesterday.

Because God is eternal, and so is her life.
Otherwise that God couldn't grow at all.
As we get old, He would get small.
But, but that's not the case, or I wouldn't have had to face
That my God needed to grow.

Because through the trinkets in her house, through the faded blouse,
my God continued to grow.
Because with each story of days long ago Came the pain,
the remorse and the show
Of the incredible kindness of a loving Father who tenderly extended
His hand during episodes in her life as it was all within His plan
And, my God grew yesterday. I'm here to say.
Because she walked me through her life, year by painful year.
A step at a time she told me the rhyme.
How her image of God had grown.

And, she showed me through her eyes the faithfulness of His
Who cared for her all along
It wasn't her wits, her friends, her education which made her strong
But grace along, had come to shown.
Her how to survive in the face of defeat and pain,
God had brought her gain Grace came through
Where there was none at all. When she was small.
My image of God grew with her yesterday.

In the face of her mother who died when she was a child
In the back of her father who deserted her later on.
In loneliness, hardships and broken relationships; love lost and spent.
My God grew yesterday.

Because, when she met her sum, and added it all up
She had found herself at the end of the trail.
Face down with a fractured hip, she could only flail.
Because no one but God knew she was there.
What despair?
Fallen, alone and crying in the brook,
she lay bent broken and completely shook.
And cried out to God.
So my image of God grew yesterday.

Because, she tells me somehow, she knew.
The same God from before, That God she grew had grown to be her
friend, as the days passed on by
watching the years fly

And, she just knew
He would not let her die as she lie
Face down in the mud at the end of the trial.
She put up her sail and billowed out to Him.
And, He responded to her plea
It wasn't just a whim
And He plucked her from the mud and carried her safely home.
That God that grew; She got Him on the phone.

But how did she know?
That is the mystery at hand
That God could bring help to her side
How did she know.
Did She abide? I think so.
And I'll tell you the truth.
Lord God Almighty is not only for the youth.
He loves us all, and especially those grown old.
I know it for myself, today
Not merely something I'm told.

For that image of God can only
Grow when watered and fed day by day as we are led.
Held in His hand, threaded through His plan.
This God of All. Surely He can And He does.

June 15, 2006

Written on the plane on the way home from taking care of my grandmother who had fallen and fractured her hip. I cared for her the week following her surgery.

Introduction to Palms of Love:

I gave my all and saved his life.
They are aghast that one is so passionate about her job.
And, I am, as well.
So, where did all this passion come from?
Sent from above, the love from the Dove.

And, I stripped chest tubes pulling blood clots from his chest to prevent the blood from building up around his heart which could cause suffocation of his heart. I pulled at the clots in the chest tubing for two hours with my bare hands and saved his life. Then I wrote: Palms of Love.

Later, the next week I presented the piece to his family who ordered some of my books and changed their life seeing God in a new way.

Palms of Love

Unveiled, unclothed, undone. Open, extended, barren. Upright palms,
I extend to You my Savior.
Callous, worn, bruised, torn.
Upright palms I extend to You, my Lord. Emit, commit, and submit, I
give my hands to You, My Lord, I open my plans.
Holding tight, with all my might,
I have clung to what is mine.
I release it now. To You I give this vow. Upright palms I extend to You,
My Savior. Through the night, bring Your light.
Show the way. Become my say.
Fill me to full. I cease from my pull.
I give You the rope. Give me the Hope.
My desire, my yearn, my dream, let me to learn.
Open hands extended, I reach
from my heart to Yours, come, Lord, teach these upright palms to
extend to others.
To reach to those who are my brothers
to love the way only You know,
to give compassion grown to show
strength in my palms that comes from above
from the God, the Father, the creator of love.

Brought on Through

And will you bring me through? I did. And, will you bring them
through? That is the reason I brought you through.
For, by your hand, they will come.
You have opened the door to
understanding dreams.
And I am going
to put you on
the front page of
every
newspaper
in the world.
I am going to put My glory on the front page
of everywhere.
Watch and see. I will
rise. Thank you, for,
you
were willing to sit down, take a back seat and
let Me drive. And, I have driven you like a sheep with my rod.
I exalt You, Oh God Most High. I lift my spirit to Your presence Be
exalted in my life, through my fingers
bring life to Your voice. And, it
did happen, didn't it?
Hallelujah!
I have been threaded through the
hiding place
to see the light.
 Like going through the
middle of the rock, He led me
through the places of darkness. Lord,
I praise You, Oh God Most High, Be exalted!
Hallelujah! You have mined through solid Stone
to reach the other side. Amazing light has been turned on.

Left-Handed Christians

Left-handed people aren't wrong, they are just left handed.
They use the other hand to do things that others don't.
They are different. And, they are born that way.
So, no matter what we do, they continue to be different.
We cannot train them to be the same as everybody else,
because they are not.
Likewise, we cannot train all the people in Church to use the same
hand. They will use the other hand sometimes.
And what will be do? Slap them?
To us, when we use the right hand,
it seems right. But, to use the left hand, seems wrong.
Left is not wrong. It is different.
The same purpose is accomplished, but the method is different.
There are many sharing the good things of God differently from us, do
we slap them?
We shouldn't.
Just because it is different does not mean it is wrong.
Maybe they were born left-handed.

Lot's Wife

When we continue to focus on something that God has taught us long ago, then we are stuck in a season. The Spirit of God is a River, not a lake; He flows, is not stagnant. When we come across a profound truth, just like finding a diamond in the sand, sometimes we may have a tendency to elevate that truth above all others and put it as central in our life. This is not God's intention. The truth was a diamond given to you at that time and it was meant to be the most important thing for you to learn then, but that same thing won't continue to be the most important thing forever. God wants to teach us. Part of learning is moving from one level to another. When you find a diamond put it in your pocket. From that vantage point you are able to pull it out again and again and focus on it when you need encouragement. Don't make a diamond ring out of it.

The reason you should not make a diamond ring out if that diamond is because you are not the teacher. How do you know when the lesson is finished? Perhaps you have just received chapter three of the book; and now you close the cover and mount it on the wall. You see, when you close the cover on the book; or stop at that specific teaching, then you have, in essence, mounted the diamond. And, after the diamond is mounted, it is difficult to change the setting. To change a setting of a diamond, the prongs must be broken or bent and they will never be able to be used again. You have ruined a mounting. Maybe that diamond is meant to join others to become a sparkling necklace. How do you know?

You don't.

Think of it like this: Suppose God gives you an amazing revelation. This is something that you have wondered about for a long time and; just like that, God places a teaching into your heart. It is like flour.

Then, again, the next month, God gives another amazing insight into something you never knew before. Think of it like eggs. Oh, then again the next week God shows you something in the environment which brings an awesome lesson. Think of it like baking soda. Do you see? We are gathering the ingredients to bake something. Not sure what, just yet, but I notice that we are gathering. And, as you move along, God continues to give you wondrous teachings. How do you know when to put them together? When He says so. Get it? Because if we stop short of the final teaching, we may end up attempting to bake a cake without salt. Oh, you say, salt is such a little thing, how important could that be?

Salt is, probably the most important ingredient to your whole recipe because salt is what gives rise to the season. If we gather our ingredients and bake our cake, yet bring it to the wrong party, we will be found in error. Oh, but you say: I will keep it with me all the time, that way I will be always ready: in essence you are bringing your cake to every party. What if it's not a party? What if you are going to a funeral? Would you bring a birthday cake to a funeral? Certainly not.

You see, we can, even, wait on God to provide all of the ingredients we need, then wait on Him to help us put the cake together, yet still have problems with presentation because we show up in the wrong place at the wrong time. How important is the season?

I can't remember Lot's wife's name. Can you? I think there is a reason I can't remember her name and it's because she represents something I would rather not become. What happened to Lot's wife is that when God sent angels to rescue Lot from a bad situation, she had regrets. He focused on what God had built in her life before, rather than being willing to move into the promises which lay ahead. She had a hold of a diamond which she had found in the past. She had mounted that diamond and built her life around it: It was her home. She had built her life around her family, her community and her house.

Take note women. She had built her house and 'settled down' so, when it was time to move, she wasn't ready to go. Remember, moving in the Holy Spirit is a River, not a lake. So, God made her to be what she represented: That season. She became salt. She was stuck in that season, so as she demonstrated her inability to move with Him, He couldn't use her. You see, even if He hadn't turned her into to a pillar of salt, she would have been a hindrance to the mobility of the entire group because she was stuck; she had seen God build her dreams and was unable to let go of them when He called her to another purpose.

God calls us from one place to the next, He is building a cake. He had a much greater purpose with Lot and his family than to settle down in Sodom.

Remember, we are supposed to be 'passers' in this world, not 'settle down' and get comfortable. Is our purpose to make ourselves comfortable? I think that is the primary issue: What is your purpose?

When we assume that we know our purpose and we see a glint of it coming true, we have a tendency to grasp and hold it tight. Then, we get 'blue knuckle syndrome' hanging onto that purpose (it's only the flour of the cake). And, when our hands are full hanging onto that purpose, they are not empty to accept another purpose which is the next step along our path in our walk toward the ultimate purpose of giving glory to God. If we live by the Spirit, we need to get into step with the Spirit.

Threads of Mercy

Threads of mercy, threads of light threaded through
my spirit tonight. Stitched and sewn, enlightenment
shown threaded
through my spirit tonight.
Threads of purpose bind my soul.
A matrix of magic meant for
within inside my being
is where He begins to
thread His mercy
and spin His light.
Effervescent
echoes on
through
the
Threads of
mercy true be to
you Indeed,
in love,
in might through and
through. A weaving holiness to unity
from me to you, then, returned all at once
just like before threads of mercy opens the door.

Four Dream Tapestry

This is actually four dreams which I had in the same night. They are interwoven, so I will give the dreams then the interpretation of them. Weaving the four dreams puts you in the 'advanced' dream interpretation understanding classification. We are on page 112 in the last chapter of book 7 in the series of Steps in the Garden {if you have been following along}, so by now you should be ready to weave.

Washing Cars-Dream 1:
We're all soaping down our cars because the neighborhood car wash is coming around. Then some guys come by with a car on fire. We turn the hose on and it has incredible pressure and nobody needs to hold it. This amazing hose that carries the water under pressure practically brings itself to those who need fire control. It goes to the place where they are. As the men with the car on fire drive by, they grab the hose and put their fire out. But, the fire rekindles. Those of us standing in the street realize that we must be quick if we are going to keep this fire under control.

Room for others-Dream 2:
They have given the children their grandmother's house. They have a roof over their head, but the hose is in disrepair. In fact, if you worked on it, you could see where this house could be made for more than one to live in. It could be split in two parts because there is room for others. Yet, I notice that the floor is very weak Because this structure is in disrepair and very old, I cringe at the thought of what's under these floor tiles. I am sure there is rottenness in the foundation. I can see that in this grandmother's house, the furniture is usable but the foundation is bad. He is a student.

Spiritual Relief-Dream 3:
And I went to my daughter and found her crying. They were trying to soothe her but didn't know what the problem was. So, I took her to the bathroom. I relieved her. They didn't know how to release what was pent up within her. It is all in the area of cleansing. She did fine when she went there on her own without them. I was wondering if it would work, but it did.

Eager to Learn-Dream 4:
There is one that is eager to learn the things of God. He doesn't have much by way of possessions. Everything fits inside his car, so the family has tried to help him out. They gave him their parent's house to live in. It's OK that things are old, but the problem lies in the sturdiness of the original building. Generation after generation they have built in the teaching of their forefathers. But who dares to tear down the building and the foundation to see if it's sturdy. They reason the building is already up and the structure in place, so why rebuild it? But, what if there is nothing but dirt under this weak floor?

Interpretation:
To interpret these dreams together, first we must step back from the 'canvas' and decide what the subject is. I would say that they all have some common threads.

Teaching in the Church Students

Coming to rely upon old things which are passed down.

Cleansing and washing

Let's Weave

Taking *dream 1* about washing cars, we can correlate vehicles with gifts which God has given us. For example: One of the gifts which God has given me is interpretation. The vehicle which He is presently using to 'carry' this gift is writing. I have a truck which hauls these lines to you. In essence I have a 'line hauler' called writing. My writing needs to be cleansed; washed, and purified to be able to use it for the glory of God. In order for us to be used as a conduit to share the fruits of the Holy Spirit, we need to clean pipes. Whatever gunk that is built up, needs to be cleaned out. We need to come to God and ask for regular cleansing through the blood of Jesus. {There is no other cleansing available.} Then, we need to drop our weights at His feet.

Only then will our hands be free to do whatever He needs done. If our hands are dirty and full, God can't use them for His work. I go to that place often: In fact what He has told me is that I'm kind of like a woman on a camping trip in that I stop by every sink I can find along the way and clean up. I don't wait to get really dirty, or for a 'special' time of reconciliation, but seek it often.

Back to the dream:

As we soap down the vehicle, He has given us, He will bring cleaning through our work. Why do we wait for the corporate car wash when He has placed the house in our own front yard?

In the dream there was also, a fire on a flatbed truck that the enemy rolled down the street close to our vehicles putting them in danger of destruction. But, the 'washer truck' took out the fire that was slated to destroy our vehicles and homes. Notice the wording of the dream: The water came with incredible pressure and the hose didn't need to be directed to respond to the need. *God's Holy Spirit knows how to meet our needs for cleansing and to help destroy the enemies in our lives.*

The dream has another message. It speaks about the people in this neighborhood and how they learn about the washing which is done by the 'big washer'. At first, they try to wash their own cars, but then they learn that the washer truck will come through and wash all of them exactly as they need it.

Dream 2 is about giving the grandson his grandmother's house with a rotten foundation. The central message is that "If the foundation isn't any good, why build on it?"

I would challenge 'the student' to study their foundation and ask God to reveal what their foundation is made of. Just because the house was given to you, doesn't mean that it is good. *That is the message of the dream.* What that means is that if you have received teaching from forefathers, it may be rotten under the floorboards.

This dream speaks about sturdiness in the building. Often, we refuse to tear down a building because it is old. Nostalgia in religion is alive and well. To keep bad teaching because 'we have the structure already in place' is not pleasing to God.

Dream 3 is about a crying daughter that I take to the bathroom. The crowd didn't seem to be able to fix her. What she needed to do was go to the bathroom. Often, in dreams, when someone goes to the bathroom, she needs relief and to release that which is waste. The Church crowd wasn't able to do it, where I was able to do it one on one. I believe the message in this dream is that individuals need to seek their own cleansing and relief apart from the central worship time.

Dream 4 gives the picture of someone eager to learn the things of God. He is needy and goes to the Church. They give him the structure that their forefathers used. This dream says that a structure is only as good as its foundation. What if the foundation is dirt? That would be in contrary to Spirit. What the man is looking for is a spiritual foundation and what if the old structure provides a physical foundation without a Spirit? Remember, that a spiritual foundation must be on God's Holy Spirit, not on sound teaching, doctrine, or Religion.

To weave the dreams together, the central message is that Church is good if it is built on a foundation inspired by the Holy Spirit. We need to be willing to build new structure using fresh foundation in our teaching and not be sequestered into using structure just because 'we always do it this way'.

In addition, the dreams all speak of the individual nature of God's Holy Spirit to speak to us in a way that corporate Religion can't. In the first dream, the Spirit {water truck} cleanses the vehicles and douses the enemy who would destroy the entire neighborhood. In the second dream, we are challenged to let God show us our foundation. In the third dream, the Spirit knows the girl's sin and helps her to find relief. Then, in the last dream, the Spirit wants to lead individuals to learn rather than see them follow structure which may have a bad foundation.

The First is Last

I've been on the front now another stepped in front of me. She was out of order.

She didn't know it before, but now she does. The permission starts from the back and I am the last one now. There was another there but she became inpatient and couldn't wait her turn.

She stepped on me as she passed by in front of me. I would have moved before now, but I paid attention to the whole order not just what was going on in my own chair. Now I realize that I have waited for all to proceed ahead so I will become last.

But that makes me to be first in the kingdom of God because when you are in front you are the last one to receive. You can be assured that you will not be forgotten.

Team Leaders

It's a track, a trail, a move out front of the team
Someone needs to take the ball and break from the pack
Will it work, I'm not sure. Danger will lurk, but I will not shirk To break from the pack is sure to cause some flack
But, if no one takes the lead, how can others follow?

If no one steps out, we will continue to be with doubt Doubt in our ability, in the power of the words of our God to lead
because a team isn't led by a ball, by a score, or a free-for-all.

By a captain in charge, not everyone making themselves large And, who dares to assume the lead and grasp the ball,
stretch out in front and give it their all?

Certainly not the goalie, the kicker or the tight end, I contend It is he who is chosen by the Captain of them all
Who stretches out his faith hoping he won't fall.
Were his lessons all done? Did he complete his run?

Did he pay attention in class to be ready to run this dash? Can his hope be sure? Is his vision pure?
Will he make it to the goal? Let us cheer him on. Does he have what it takes to bring the others, to the point of dawn?
Will they follow, take their cue?

Are they paying attention to themselves or you?
Do they stare down their own shirt?
gaze at their own name tag? Or, will they join the race,
entering with the team without any lag?

For, what is a leader if no one joins the team? How can they play if it doesn't seem that they work together to achieve a common goal?

That we might all assume our role, our positions in the place That we will know where we belong along this life's race. Help us, Dear Lord to know where we belong Because in You, alone, we are free.

And, give us eyes to recognize the leaders of the team
That we might pass the ball, tip our serve and forever redeem
Those that need it.

Because it is good to know that we were there
when we needed to be in the right place according to the Lord.

Held in His Affection
{A song}

To be in love with someone who can do anything is amazing.
To be held within His affection is beyond my grasp.

Heavenly Redeemer, forever true, came from the sky to you.
Be my delight, light my fire.
Demonstrate Your might, stop Satan's conspire.

God of mercy, God of love,
sent from Heaven, the doom above.
Reign down Your mercy, shower the love.
Hail to the King, love from above.

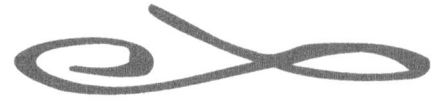

Rock Through the Window

Up, up and away flies my intentions with my word unhindered by anything in this earth. And, who can stop wind? Who can hold out his hand and harness it?

Only God above, who lives within.

Certainly, when you raise your hand, and speak my intentions, the wind stills. But, it still needs to be my intentions.

See, you, my dear, have stumbled upon something amazing.

It is the rock that others trip over, you use to take out windows. You have shattered kingdoms of the enemy with the rock in your hand. For, by the force of my words, my power goes forth to achieve grace. The rock, Jesus, is the one who goes through.

But, who would have thought about tossing Him through windows? Most coddle Him and tuck Him into their pocket. Others set Him on a window sill and in a garden.

They hold Him dear, put Him into their garments, admire Him, and set Him on display in their intimate places.

They wear crosses with private meanings of personal victories. Still, others trip over Him day after day, like a bump along the path.

They don't know how to use the Christ of cleansing.

But, who would have thought that He could be tossed through a window.

A window of understanding the voice of God. A window to seeing God for who He really is.

They assumed the window was part of the wall. It was so fogged over, that nobody could see through it.

Had it been soaped over long ago? Had it been bricked from the outside? Indeed.

So, I un-piled the bricks, broke down the mortar of the enemy, then picked up the rock and tossed it through the widow. It wasn't easy because it involved wounding Christ.

How could I possibly deliberately crush Him once more? How could I put My Savior to the test?

But, I realized that this was intended. He planned it that way from the start. He is the one who is to go through the window.

Did we think that He would crawl through it?

Did we think that He would open the window from the inside? How

could He? He came from this side like us.
But, He is God, you say, He can open the window.
But, we cannot rewrite a plan that has been written since eternity past.
He was wounded for our transgressions.
He took on our infirmities.
And, does He continue to take them? Indeed.
So, does He continue to be wounded?
No, once and for all, He laid down His life for us. But, we still need to go there.
We need to face the cross, go through the nail wounds and allow that point of suffering to happen again in order for us to have victory.
It is by His stripes that we are healed. He bore our sins on the cross, so that we might live.
And, do we continue to live? Yes, we do.
Does He continue to bare the sins?
Yes. Do we think that we are doing Him a favor by not allowing Him to bare them?
And, I ask, does He notice when He bares our sins?
Does He continue to feel the pain, the agony, the disgust?
I think so.
But, just like a woman in childbirth, the pain is momentary compared to the birth of a new life. For, each time we come to Him and lay our burdens on Him, He bares them. It does cause Him pain, but He is built to endure it. Just like the woman who bares the child, He is ready. It is His joy to bare us in order to deliver us. And, the rock? It's Him. He is the one who we grasp. For, when we thoroughly grasp why He came, and the purpose of His mission, then we won't be afraid to make use of the provision. We really don't have anything else to use that will get us through the window.
God has provided Jesus.
When we grasp Him, then we pray in the power of the Holy Spirit, He is moved. His heart is moved toward His Fathers'.
Is not the Father on the other side of the window? Certainly, there is a veil between us and God. It is a window that we see dimly through to understand spiritual things.
But, you see, if we grasp what Jesus
came for, then we will not be afraid to use what He has provided.
We will pick up the rock and use it. Use the forgiveness daily, the cleansing, deliverance, healing, and Salvation.

But. Who would have thought to use the rock to break the window between God and us? For, when I broke the window I could see God's face. He didn't move, only I could see Him, now. And, hear Him, too.

Hail to the King
{A song}

Held by a hand I cannot see
bound by a heart I have been set free.
Praise the Lord, I give my praise to Thee.

Held by a hand I cannot see
Tenderly caressed by a loving arm.
He holds me tight keeping me from harm.
Praise the Lord, I give my praise to Thee
Glory to You, Father, Son, Spirit, Three.

Spirit of Truth, set my heart on fire
Teach me to blaze in front; light a mighty choir.
That lifts their voices to You, to sing Your praise
Counting You worthy, their voices together they raise.

Held by a hand we cannot see
Led by a voice he has set us all free to be
Alive to sing, our voices we bring
Hallelujah to Him, hail to the King.

My Caëfa

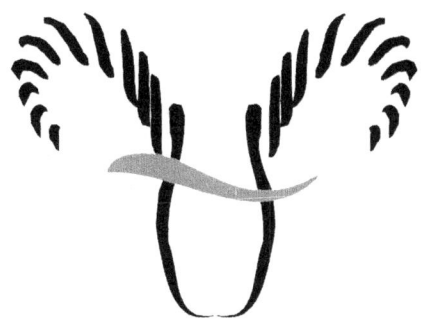

Capitulate: Surrender to His ways and summarize subject.
Associate: Connect with Him having subordinate status.
Emulate: Compete for the answer. Vie for the truth against all else.
Facilitate: Make it easy and convenient. Ask and write it down.
Appreciate: Become fully aware of the value; to be sensitive to and show gratitude for with an increase in proportionate value to that which is revealed. It's OK to say, "Thanks.

The first time I used Caëfa acronym was in the book Dreamatrix Immanuel. I demonstrated how God gave me dreams and I was able to derive the meaning which became useful to me. It is like telling a testimony. With these kinds of books, I can tell the dreams and the Scriptures with their interpretations, but something clicks when I demonstrate how I put it all together to make it work for me. When I share the Caëfa it is personal insight which I feel He has given to me. I merely share it in the hope that it will help you, as an individual, figure out some things on your own which are important to your growth in intimacy toward God.

Consequently, I tack the Caëfa on the end of the book as an addendum of 'this is how I got what I got and this is what I did with it.
I feel God has threaded me through to His promises by faith relying upon His words to bring about this marvelous ministry of sharing dreams and visions in books. He showed me the foundation of the business and fed me with the strategy for how to run it His way, and then I walked into it.
To me it has been like growing into a pair of shoes which I see set out in front of me. Only now, as I complete this book, have I been threaded completely from one side of the needle to the other on a

wing and a prayer. Only last week did I obtain printing equipment and the ability to correlate many of the ideas which He gave me a long time ago. Only last week did I have the money to pay the bills, yet have twice the stuff. He multiplied what I needed by His hand. It has been like bread in a bowl for me; each time I look in the bowl, there continues to be more provision for today.

The pieces that follow in this section are personal. They show my struggle and demonstrate how I cling to the promises seeking His affirmation to complete His words. I believe I will begin by showing a dream He gave me last night:

Pure Vessel

The dream:
There is a boat that my husband bought. The reason he wanted this boat was that it had never been boarded from the shore using the ladder, but always from the dock. No one had put any dirt on the sides of the fresh white boat. And, I get into the boat and my husband uses me to mark the route along the way tossing anchors at crucial spots.

Interpretation:
A boat is the gifting which God uses to 'float' His ministry which He has given to me. I didn't use a ladder to get into the place which He paid the price to provide for His wife {the Church}. I never tried to climb into the boat on my own because I didn't know how. When I came to the Holy Spirit, it was a completely new experience for me. I wasn't raised in an environment which teaches about the gifts of the Spirit or Tongues, or any of the things which He has given me dreams and instruction to share in the books with others. I came without any preconceived ideas because I didn't have any.

In another vision, He showed before that religious strongholds can be like the waves of the ocean which come against someone as he tries to wade out to get onto a boat. It is very difficult to walk out from the shore and get into a boat because the waves push you back to the place where you came from. Religious ideas which are contrary to what God wants to teach you Himself, make it very difficult to enter into the 'craft' which He wants to provide to keep the gifts of the Spirit afloat. Four years ago when I ended up in a small charismatic Church, I heard that someone could receive the Holy Spirit. A friend of mine obtained a book which discussed the baptism of the Spirit and we read it eagerly, together peeking over one another's shoulder while at work. Then, I timidly approached one of the elders and asked if we could become baptized in the Spirit. He told me that in three months they would have a meeting and baptize us. My friend and I prayed and fasted waiting for the day of our baptism. I remember that before the actual service, she asked the same elder who promised to share the baptism of the Spirit with us to pray for her sick sister. We joined hands in the hallway with him and his wife as they prayed for her sister.

And, after the prayer, my friend leaned down and whispered into my ear, "Did we receive the Spirit? Was that it?"

We had no idea what it meant to become baptized in the Spirit. To finish the story, that night the Pastor invited anyone who wanted to receive the baptism of the Spirit to be prayed over and they came up front toward the altar and were prayed over. I officially received the baptism of the Spirit November 19th, 2001.

But, what this dream means to me is that I never had any ideas of what was to be expected when I entered the 'craft' so I had to do it His way.

When I asked God to interpret the dream for me today, this is what He said:

The difference with you, Sheri, is that you refused to do it yourself. You emptied your heart and hands, and then waited for the fulfillment of the promise. How I love you.

You didn't let the experiences of others taint your earnest desire to seek Me. You screamed at the air and demanded a response. – And that is the most remarkable thing; To demand a response from the Almighty God. But you studied to prove yourself true; you purified your soul and sanctified your heart. You cleansed every area of your life washing through the blood, kicking out evil, the world and the flesh. You did your homework, girl, I'll say that much.

The amazing thing is that you approached Me in anticipation of meeting Me and having Me meet you. And, Oh wouldn't our prayer be different if we saw God face to face each time we prayed?

I think if I was to say that you have keys that I would say that it is a combination you have found which unlocks the vault of God's heart.

For, in your hand are keys and in My hand are the rest. The keys you hold are the desire for purity, honesty, reverence, humility, and honor of God above yourself. You hold the keys to reject the world's views, religious mediocrity or strife, your flesh and demonic influence. Those keys are yours.
And, Sheri, I only have one key; the power and authority to make it happen. By your desire and My ability the vault opens to release My desire and your ability. We hold hands and walk.

It is when they assume to hold hands with Holiness having unwashed hands that it becomes impossible.

In Love

I'm in love with someone I don't really know.
I can't tell you where He's from and he doesn't seem to have any parents.
He doesn't ever leave to go to work, yet has pockets bulging with cash every day. But, I love Him so, I quit being worried.

I'm in love with someone I don't really know.
I don't really mind that He intrudes on my personal time; I decided to invite him to everything.
Because whether or not in want, He's always got an opinion about things others don't care about. But, I love Him so, I quit being worried.

I'm in love with someone I don't really know.
I can tell you the day we met; there was joy in the air. And, we've been friends ever since.
Without fail, He comes to my house daily and we chat; hour after hour on the bed, on the couch, in the tub.
He has certainly seen me at my worst, yet I've quit being worried.

I'm in love with someone I don't really know, Yet it seems like we have been friends forever.
He was there when I was young, and is there until now
Watching, waiting and wondering when we will spend time together.
And, we do.

I'm in love with someone I don't really know
But, I can tell you the color of His eyes and how His cheeks move when He smiles.
And, I know Him so well, that I can tell when He's about to roll with laughter
I know Him. And, I'm in love.
I'm swooned, enthralled, rapt and totally entangled with His heart
And, I don't mind.
You lie.
You do mind.
Over, above, beyond and through
I have been in love with you. You're there too.
The tears on your pillow have turned Me into a weeping willow. You mind. Mounting wings as eagles we have flown from mountain top to mountain top soaring from tree top to tree top amidst the misting morning. Our wings glistening in the sun as the snow reflected along the con trail. You mind.
Wing tip to wing tip we flew like jet fighters up and over mountains of issues. Prayer after prayer, battle after battle, we have eyed the situation together and claimed victory. .. and won.
And the side you see is the one next to you. The other is for later on.
Like an eagle flying next to you, you see the side facing you.
And, that is what you know. It's enough.

Joining Spirits

He was terminal, so I tried to bring him comfort. But, he was too worried about what others thought to relax in the relationship. He was worried about going public that all would know about our intimacy.

How can I help him if he won't cooperate.

And there was a woman going to the same place as me, so I thought we could stick together. But, she was too busy for my companionship.

There is a terminal aspect of God's Kingdom on earth. It ends at some time. He has tried to show others about the need to be intimate with Him, but they have been too worried about being transparent in their relationship with Him to be able to stick with the job. They were fine accepting healing and comfort from Him on an intimate level, but were not willing to go public with it.

And, there are others who are going the same direction as me, but they are too wrapped up in their own notions to join with me.

Some won't want to go public with their relationship with God and others won't want to pause from their business long enough to commune within the family of God. It's a family business, remember?

It's the end of the world. Three years ago the voice was not oriented to them, so they didn't notice. Now when you talk, they will know and be repentant.

The voice needed an interpreter for them to be able to follow it. You have become an interpreter.

And, take Him home. He wouldn't eat anything, even though he was hungry. Mom was upset at his behavior.

Show the children where the food is and that it's OK to eat. Mother Wisdom wants to feed her children. Show the children where the table is within the house of God. It's a table of presence within the place where God dwells.

Inform and demonstrate: be one picture. You are the frame and the movement of the voice of God is the action. As you move by the power of the Holy Spirit, you become a motion picture that has been framed by My honor.

There was only one Spirit, but they were off doing their own thing and refused to commune with one another. There is supposed to be a communing of spirits.

God is calling me to join the family of God at His Holy Spirit. He is the one who brings about communion of the Saints according to His Spirit. They think that God is divided into several spirits because that is all that they have seen. But, they are selfish and looking to their own interests, rather than others. They have not realized that the other spirits that the others are seeing are also part of Me. Spirit of evangelism is Mine, Spirit of generosity is Mine, Spirit of Grace is Mine, Spirit of demonstration of power is also Mine. These are gifts of the same Spirit that are not meant to be separated. They need to be brought together like at Christmas and placed under the same tree of life. All of them need to appreciate the whole of My character. AM I divided? Yet, they have divided Me because they are a hand, they think I am only made of hands.

He was so worried about what the public thought that he didn't allow himself to enjoy true closeness with Me. The other problem was that he didn't want to be found out of order. His fear of authority of men overshadowed his needs for intimacy and communion.

Hike July 19, 2005

Did you ever think that you are not encountering spider webs stretched across your trail because someone is in front of you breaking the trail, being your shield from danger? Thank Him sometime for the lack. How we thank for the gain, but we fail to notice the lack of adversity.

Notice the color of the ribbon you hold in your hand. No red or rainbow, but reflective like foil. Covenants, bows of reflection bind this package. Red, yellow, blue, pink, and green. All reflective of the ones I make to God mirror from the blazing flame of the Holy Spirit.

Adoration Lift

Praise You Father of love
Praise You Heavenly Lord, above. Holy Spirit,
I lift my adoration to You On the wings of the Dove, You flew.
Praise You Father of Love
Amazing grace sent from above
Thread Your love through my heart.
Come and stay, never depart.
God of mercy, God of love
Praise to You from below to above.

Beyond your aspire, your perspire, your conspire.
Beyond your respire is My desire.

Contemplate
Associate
Translate
Communicate
Contemplate My ideas, associate them to your life. Translate them with obedience.

Meditate on my faithful provision and tell others about it. It's obedience to truth that births testimony.

Who ever said that the pathway to holiness with God on earth is straight? I find that day after day I turn things over to Him. Along the windy road as it climbs the mountain where He lives there are ups and downs. There are areas of construction. At times I am way too close to the edge and I attempt to stay on the road when I round the bends. It is comforting to know that if I go over the edge, He will bring His tow truck to haul me back on to the path of righteousness.

Telepathic Fishing

The ideopathetic telepathic steps from reason to not. She is like a dock. She goes as far as she can safely step, and fishes for the rest. Taking your need, she dangles her bait, smiggins of what you need. Her aim is to snag you, reel you in and feed you just enough to make you return for more. She lures with curiosity for things not yet known. Does she know the future? Not hardly. She's just fishing at a dead end place.

Risen from Shattered

I would like a new name, please, Lord. Your new name is 'Risen'
Shattered, crushed and beaten down, I found my victory on my face when I emptied my hands and cleaned my heart. There was a terrible bloody battle. I was left with fractures and bruises and when I fell down, the foot of Satan was on my chest with his spear poised ready to pierce me through. So, I turned over and cried out to God, then waited for Him to rescue me. And amazing thing happened. When I opened my eyes, he was gone. What I found was merely a shadow of death had taunted me. And, the tape was removed from the mouths of the cheering section when I stood up. They feared the worse and were held speechless. But, I have stood. I have risen from the dead. Sure, I am bruised and limp about, but I am up and have found that there is now no opponent that can stand against me. He has left because the truth has been declared and triumphed over him. My Father has whispered the victory to me. Praise Him!
And, once more we have learned an important lesson about fighting an invisible opponent. Hit the floor, face down, earlier in the match and trust your heart when it's held in God's hand.
Just because it has a mean face, doesn't mean the back side is hard to climb. Check the back door. It may be open.
Sometimes we go up the face of the rock. We take out the ropes, hooks and screws and mount a mission to go straight up the steepest part of the mountain. And, sometimes, God will be our hiking partner accompanying us up the most intimidating place of bony peaks. Why does He go that way when the other way is so much easier?

It's a power demonstration to show others that training in exercise and teamwork develop agility. And, isn't it inspiring to see that climb straight up the face of the mountain dangling by the rope, supported on a single swivel loop?

But, He is your partner and He has made this climb thousands of times. Climbing the mountain of prayer and praise through teamwork and obedience in training and stamina. It is a powerful demonstration of what a whole hearted person is worth to God.

Sheri, what you pass on is dried bread. They just add water.

Its like trail mix. Freeze dried fruits and nuts. Fruits of the Holy Spirit and evidence that is bursting from the shell.

All of the above I received on this hike on the same day. I just wrote it down to share it with you today.

My Testimony

God has thoroughly confirmed in my spirit that He has given me assignments along with His power and Presence to do it. This is my study of it. I feel led to make detailed notes because I know the devil. He circles back causing doubt. My goal is to give no advantage to him, and to ever give the Glory to God. After careful study of the scriptures and several books, I feel that God has confirmed in my spirit the answers that I asked for. He has given me the gift of Mercy which has blossomed into several other gifts as He has called them into action for His purposes. It has been a building process. Because of my disciplined background, I refused to acknowledge any gift until it was fully grounded in the Scriptures.

As a Young Child

I was born in Seattle, Washington. My mother had divorce my father by the time I was old enough to remember anything. (I was 4). My earliest memories are pleasant. We went to Catholic Church. I received my First Holy Communion at age 5. We would go to Church faithfully and I would wear a doily on my head and nice white gloves. Then, my mother got caught up in doing volunteer work on the military base and fell in love with another man. The Catholic Church told her not to come anymore. That was the last time I went to Church until I was 16. My mother subsequently was married 5 times. I was moved so many times during my childhood that my school transcript shows 14 schools in 12 years. Two of the step-fathers sexually abused me over a period of years. My mother never knew about it...I kept it a dark ugly secret.

Although I never thought we were poor, I remember that I never had a new dress until I was 17 years old. Usually I slept on a mattress on the floor and had a box for my clothes. Several times we were forced to leave everything we owned and move. My mother was always looking for somewhere that she 'heard' was better. Then we would get there and find out that it was usually worse. Consequently, I grew up a 'scarred' young girl with a lot of dark secrets. I was very happy when someone told me about a Savior who would be your friend and never leave you. I remember that the day I received Jesus when I went home, the sexual abuse stopped. God came into my world and rescued me.

My Early Salvation Years

When I was 16 years old, I found myself attending a Christian High School. There, at an event, I walked forward and received Christ as my personal Savior. I went to a Baptist Church and got involved in Campus Crusade of Christ Ministries. There was a group of very disciplined Christians that I joined with, the Navigators. They prided themselves with memorizing scripture. I memorized over 100 scriptures in the next two years to complete their highest level program. I received a scholarship to go to a Bible College and went for one year. I ran out of money and had to come home. My parents were divorcing at this time, so I chose to join my boyfriend in Oregon while he finished College. He lived in the dormitory and I lived in an old house with five Christian girls. I got married at a young age to a Christian man I met at a Bible Camp while I was working there during the summer. We waited until he graduated from College (3 years) and were married. We maintained our virginity through this time and gave our Christian Testimonies at the wedding ceremony. We were 'perfect Christians'. I was given 5 showers by different groups of women.

We were loved by many. I can't tell you how many people I have let to salvation. I would talk to anybody that would listen. It wasn't unusual for me to get on a bus, lead someone to Christ and get off of it without even learning their name. I was the first one in my family to Come to Christ and now all are saved and my two brothers went to

Bible College for the ministry. My husband joined the military and we continued to join with very disciplined Bible groups. We did not have a television because we did not want the outside influence of the word. We memorized the book of Philippians together as a unity project. We thought that we were doing everything right. I would spend exactly 8 minutes praying, 17 minutes reading the scriptures, and 4 minutes each day writing down what God told me from the verses. This was my communication with God during those years. It was a dry, disciplined march that I was committed to do because it was right. We went along for a number of years until the leader of our Bible study committed suicide. Then two months later, another leader got a divorce. I was devastated and my walk with the Lord Shipwrecked. I determined that 'the God thing' doesn't work. I quit reading and praying and three years later divorced my Christian husband of 14 years.

My Abandoning years

There was a period of 17 years where I wallowed in hurt and separation from God because of my shaky foundation. I had built my foundation on others, and it fell... and the fall was great in my life.

During these years sometimes I would go to a Church. I never opened my Bible, although I still own it to this day, I never opened it then. It happened that my oldest daughter got into drugs when she turned 17.

She quickly advanced to an addition. I was panicked and knew that she needed God. He was her only hope. I didn't want Him particularly, but She sure needed Him, I thought. So I tried to get others to talk to her. I would call local churches and have the pastors talk with her.

It didn't work very well because she was usually 'high'. Everything came to a head one night when she was 'high' and I couldn't take it any longer. I loaded her and my old Bible in the car and drove for the desert. We stayed in distant hotels for 5 days while she detoxed.

I had her read Exodus to me as we drove in circles in the desert. We drove until we came to this road that is entitled, "the loneliest road in the USA'.

Out there on that stretch, she stopped and looked at me and said, "Mom, you know the answer to what will bring me peace and happiness in my life, don't you?"

I Said, "Yes."

She said, "Why don't you just say it and get it over with."

So out there in the desert, I led her to a saving relationship with Jesus Christ. And when I did, I led myself back. Because in order to lead her, I had to believe it was true for me.

On the way home, God told me, in my spirit, "I want you to go to that building, the one that you were going to set up a business in and to do My business. Go to that Church and give them $100."

Esther and I went home then. It was July 4th, and she wanted to see the fireworks. However, as soon as we got home, she used some more drugs. She was taking too long in the bathroom and I opened the door and saw the reflection of a drugs down her shirt. I wrestled them from her and she fell backwards onto the tile floor and stopped breathing.

I called 911 and started Artificial Breathing. The response time for the paramedics was 45 minutes because it was nine PM on July 4th when all of the fireworks in the City of Las Vegas go off simultaneously. God is good and He gave me the grace to do what I needed to do at the time. She went to the hospital, was revived and transferred to drug rehabilitation for a while.

The Holy Spirit

I did what God instructed me to do. I went to that Church and gave them $100. Then the next week, I gave them my piano. It was there that I learned the missing ingredient to my earlier Christian walk: The Holy Spirit.

After receiving the Holy Spirit, I determined to have a pure relationship with God, one based on my relationship with Him, His relationship with me, and His Holy Word. I determined to take the human factor out of it as much as possible. The Holy Spirit came to me with incredible power (does He have any other); but I sought to open myself up to receive as much as I could. I prayed in desire for Him. I also prayed for Him to use all of the scripture I had previously memorized ...and continued to memorize more. The gift of the Holy Spirit came to me November 2001 after 6 months of seeking and praying for more from God. Nori Wong imparted the Holy Spirit to me.

The Gift of Tongues Three months later in February, I received the gift of tongues as I drove home from work. Then, in April 2002, I received the gift of Interpretation of tongues when I went to a Holy

Spirit Meeting given by the Charismatic Catholic Assn.

They prayed over me and declared, "God has told me: You don't just love God, You are IN-LOVE with God."

After they prayed for me, I immediately got up and started praying with them as they prayed for others. They were speaking in tongues, and I started giving the interpretation of what they were saying. It was scripture.

A Burden to Pray

As I continued in obedience and prayer, I sought God in the desert. He was consistent to bring me revelations, visions, and insight into His word. I recognized the need to support the Church in prayer, so I told the Lord to wake me if He wanted me there.

He started waking me at 0400 on Sunday mornings. I began to get a burden to pray in the sanctuary. I would pray over the chairs. God started to give me visions. I would find a scripture that met the need that I saw and pray it in. I would pray over a section, and then watch what God would do with the people that would sit there. Many times, I would pray for salvation, and people would come forward for salvation as the altar call was given. One time a whole row came forward.

Seeing the Glory of God

More than a Vision: Transported to the Snow Dec 2001

I went for a hike that changed my life. There were patches of snow. I was memorizing Isaiah 1:18-19 and recognized the snow as God's covering of prayer over people. I declared that every patch of snow that I placed the imprint of my foot in was a commitment to God to pray for someone: to learn whatever I needed to be effective for His Kingdom.

The patches where there were already footprints, I proclaimed that I would encourage someone else to pray for that person or ministry.

I pursued God wildly. I asked Him to show me His Glory like He showed Moses. I selected a crevice between the mountains where I hike regularly and put Him to a test. I told no one but Him. I went on a special hike. There were patches of snow along the way. In each patch I knelt and consecrated myself to him and asked for His cleansing. I put the snow on my head, etc.

I reached the crevice and did not see His Glory, but as I started back down I found myself in what looked like a creek bed filled with large rocks/boulders of all sizes. The boulders were completely covered with snow. Ice particles were sparkling on the snow and it was powder.

The outside temperature was about 50* and it was 1030 AM. The limbs of the trees had new fallen snow on them. I climbed down through the boulders for a long time. They did not stop, but I finally climbed up through the bushes to get out. I saw the rocks covered with snow as God telling me that His vision for me was to pray for peoples after peoples because His Covering was adequate for all. (I know at this time I was transported.)

Visions in Church
Christmas Eve Service 2001 Candlelight Service.
I went to the side of the sanctuary and saw snow over everyone. Then, as pastor David ministered to individuals, I saw streamers coming down from Heaven to them. It looked like when you pour water through snow. The reflections were of gold and blue with light in the center. In January, I began to pray for Zeal for God. I started to see colors around people as they prayed, windows of Heaven during the service, and weak knees nearly every time I prayed. I found it impossible to pray sitting...I had to be on my knees. God started to give me burden to pray the Holy Spirit into the Church

A Prophecy over Me
There was a prophecy over me by DJ. Young He said, " You are the one sent for the vision for the Church as God's mouthpiece."

He said that I was in the clouds and God wanted to raise me above the clouds.

So I prayed for God to open up to me. Jan 2002 I had a vision as I sat in my living room: There was a geyser pool. It has mineral deposits around the edges. The water flows up from the bottom and there are a lot of bubbles. The water is crystal clear and pale blue, clean and pure. The view is like I have an underwater camera. There are large shadows of trees. Pine trees and other trees. Their roots touch the water. There are several trails leading to the giant geyser through the midst of the trees. The water is happy and bubbling and glad to have found the surface to be able to release the pressure. Then I found Isaiah 41:18-20.

Evidence of the Holy Spirit in my Life
I prayed for my patient at the hospital and she was instantly healed. She had internal bleeding and was comatose. Instantly, she woke up and the bleeding stopped. She was checked and all of the places where she had been bleeding had been instantly healed over.

The Call to Pray at the Hospital
Later that day God gave me an interpretation of some tongues: "I am disappointed in this hospital. People come here to get better, but many are getting worse and dieing because my people won't pray. If they would pray, then My hand would heal and they would go home instead of die."

Straight away I found an empty room that they called a 'prayer room' and started praying there. I asked God to send me someone to pray with me. I started in the first chair and asked Him to send someone by the time I came around to the kneeler bench. I would come in every day I could and sit in the next chair and pray on around the room.

Actually, by the time I go to the third chair, He sent me Helen, a Charismatic Catholic Nurse. What a wonderful time of prayer we had, then. We prayed for the hospital and for God to bring a 'real Chapel'.

Praying in a New Church Sanctuary
Sunburn in the Glory February 2002

Lana and I prayed in the New Church building. The Glory of God fell like never before. I had vision after vision and each vision; I diligently sought scripture to build a foundation to be prayed in. I didn't pray for a vision without the Word of God.

I recognized that the power was in the Scripture, not the vision. The vision was a suggestion of what to pray. Being attentive to it would bring clearer direction. Certain songs also brought in the Glory of God's presence like nothing else.

I would find myself on my face, love it and play the song over and over. My hunger for more of Him increased. Lana and I prayed about 8 hours a day for 2 weeks in between work. We got sunburn on our faces as we prayed.

Lana called a special meeting one day to pray for the financial needs of the church. She called the meeting at 5Am before I was scheduled to go to work. I showed up, but she overslept. I was found alone in the parking lot waiting for her.

I was left sitting in the dark. Not knowing what to do, I prayed the Scriptures that I felt God had given me for the Church founding. There were only about 4 verses. I had memorized them all, so it was easy.

When I prayed them in, I saw a huge beam of light come down onto the church building. It covered the whole building. I took that as God's indication that He was going to take over from here, so I went home and slept another hour before going to work.

Keys to the Kingdom of Heaven:
Dream

I had a dream. *I found a large ring of keys in my pocket. They were my step-father's keys. He had recently visited and had left them with me. He must not need them because he hadn't called for them. The keys were on a single screw with a bolt and nut, the keys threaded over the middle. I had the dream several times and realized that My Father in Heaven has left me keys.* I correlated the dream to the Bible with the help of Ron Brown. I sought to learn what the Keys the Kingdom of God are and to learn to use them.

Obedience to the dream

In March, one day when I went to work, there was a 'psychotic' patient that knew my name before I told her. I recognized that she was possessed by demons.

I asked her if she wanted to be free, and she said,' yes'. After taking authority over the demons, I led her to Christ and she became 'sane'.

Deliverance: Dream

Another dream May 2002:

'There is a small house in the tall trees. Out the window I see the base of other trees. There is only one window and one door to the house. There are two other women in the house; I do not see their faces. I am cooking something in a toaster oven on the counter. I am hungry and fixated on this thing that I am cooking in a large toaster oven. I wait and wait and the thing has skin like roasted chicken, but it isn't getting cooked. I have it on the highest temperature. So I give up and open the door and pull it out. It stands up and starts

to walk. It is the size of a small toddler. I easily grab it because it is only about the size of a two year old. It makes no sound and has no eyes or face.

It is all charred, but you can sense that the inside is not cooked and will never die. I ask the lady nearby to open the window and I grab the thing and toss it out of the window with one quick throw. Then I run quickly and lock the door and window so it cannot get back in. '

I did the best to interpret the dream. I used the information given to me in the dream to 'deliver' Esther from demonic control when she returned home being addicted to drugs. The dream was precise. At this time I had never heard of 'deliverance' and did not know about demonic activity in people's lives. I searched the scriptures for the God Base and then used the dream as an instructional booklet to guide me. I did not have one book on 'deliverance' when Esther was 'delivered'.

Esther is Healed
The Fast

April 20, 2002 the Lord told me, "It's time to heal Esther, you must walk her valley."

I had never fasted before, but God called me to it using Isaiah 58. I memorized as many verses as would fit into my head and asked four other people to join. God showed me that her deliverance was like when the paralytic was lowered into the presence of Jesus. She was paralyzed in her condition (drug addiction) and needed at least two people to take the stretcher (stretch out their hands for her), lower themselves with her into the presence of Jesus.

I went to the desert for three days and fasted and prayed continually. I prayed 90 Psalms for her. While I was out there I saw a vision of her at the foot of the Cross with her head bowed down.

I knew that when she lifted her head and looked at Jesus' face, then she would receive her healing. So, I longed to see this, but I thought I would see it in a vision. I stopped fasting after 4 days, but continued to pray for two more weeks.

Then on Cinco-de-Mayo she showed up at the end of church, in tears with everything she owned. That night, when a song was played in my living room she knelt down sobbing and turned her life over to Jesus for good. She lifted her face to Him. I knew she was healed.

She started to grow in the Lord. He showed me a vision for her. It was a large building. A tall skyscraper. Then it was blasted out from the foundation.

Vision: I was Given two ropes

June 4, 2002 Tom McGlade and I prayed in the teen room as it was opened as part of the church. God told me that the Holy Spirit is poured out, not down. It must be dispensed. As I prayed, I had a vision of two large ropes coming down to me. At first I didn't know what to do with them, but then I realized that they were for praying for the people: to bind, gather, support, heal...etc. Isaiah 60. Then God showed me not to use my hands when I pray, but to use the spirit.

God calls to me: Daughter of the Bride

June 10, 2002 the words of God came to me. He called me by a new name, 'daughter of the Bride.'

I sought God for the answer and He said that I was like Samuel.

He was a 'child of the temple'. I am to be like a 'child of the Church'. To grow up in the Church. The Bride of Christ will be my 'parent'.

I asked God to break the 'rock' of my heart into sand and make lead crystal that would reflect His Glory.

My own deliverance: heart surgery

August 2002 I went to my first Women's Encounter. I fasted. God gave me a new name; 'Honored". (I know now that means 'dream')

"For you who resists His? On the contrary, who are you, O man who answers back to God. The thing molded will not say to the molder, "why did you make me like this?' Does not the potter have a right over the clay to make from the same lump one vessel for honorable use and another for common use?"

(Rom 9:20) "I will call those who were not my people, 'my people' and her who was not my beloved, 'beloved'. (Hosea 2:23)

The Encounter was heart surgery for me. I allowed God to remove my heart, repair it and replace it with a new heart. It was so painful that it felt like having surgery without anesthesia. I looked straight into the face of those individuals that had hurt me over the years. I was returned to the times of hurt and opened my eyes to see the sin.

I received healing through asking forgiveness to people in my past. Then at the Encounter, they bound Satan and the demons and started revealing them. My demons started coming out. They called the demon out of me and told me to breathe deep x 3 and cough. When I did, a painful scream came out instead. Then my mind left me and the demons took over. It was violent; I was violent. Only for a brief time was I able to call out. My voice changed with each demon that left.

At one time, I remember being afraid for the girls that were holding me. I told them that they had better find someone bigger, because I was going to hurt them. I screamed and screamed and the demons tried to throw me on the floor, but the women spoke with authority and continued working with me until midnight.

I would black out, then come to. When I came to, I would beg them not to stop because I knew that they were in there and I wanted them out. There was a legion of demons that worked its way up out of me over a course of several hours. I first felt them in my thighs as I screamed and screamed for them to leave. They came higher and higher until they were in the back of my throat.

The demons of 'fear' and 'hate' were the last to leave. In the final attempts, I was choked by the demons and could not breathe. I saw many black hands clawing at my insides to try to stay inside. I felt my face turning purple as the demon choked me when it was called out. I was choked twice to near death before I was freed.

All of the women were praying over me harder and harder while the leader was calling out the demons. Then, I was free. My eyes became clear. Physically, I was a mess. I had wet my pants and couldn't even walk. I had to be carried to my car, but I was free!

My body was humming like all of my cells were being rebuilt in my flesh. It felt like they were all reproducing at the same time.

I listened to praise music all night and it was like God filling a swimming pool with a garden hose. I felt incredibly empty. I hummed for two days and became absorbed in praise music 24 hours a day.

I determined that they were not coming back to me, no way, no how. God was going to fill that spot. Before the Encounter when God's Glory came to me, it passed over me like a wave. After the Encounter, it felt like it passed through me. Each time the Glory passes by, all my cells start jumping for joy. It's like I am transparent. My whole body would shake.

Revelations: Demonic Spirits

God continued to show me insight into deliverance. He gave me a revelation of the spirits being like roots around your heart. They need to be unimpeded before they are cast out, otherwise it can be very painful. I sought His direction as to how to do 'surgical deliverance' rather than 'violent' deliverance. Praying for His direction and discernment first, rather than 'inciting the spirits' makes for a lot less manifestations.

The manifestations are what harms the individual in deliverance. Also, allowing the person to do their own deliverance as much as possible makes them responsible to remove the roots. He showed me how to go for the 'tap root'. The demons wrap their roots around your heart based on sin and resentment. The roots even become stone and God says that He longs to remove our stony hearts.

The branches extend and the leaves cause disability, pain and suffering. The leaves are symptoms caused by the spirits. He gave me vision of a pile of demons. They were stacked up 2x2. The higher demons suck on the lower demon's power. God showed me that if you undo them from the bottom, then you will not meet the resistance of the lead demon and by the time you get to him, he will have lost all of his power.

Since in obedience to the truth, God has purified my Soul, He has removed those nasty roots from my heart by heart surgery. Then He has replanted the seeds of His Word on the soil of my soul. It is imperishable, living, and enduring. The fruits are the fruits of the spirit and leaves are for healing. The fruit will be for food. (I Peter 1:22, Ez 47:12)

Church is Held Captive: Dream

Sept. 2002 Dream: We were held as captives in our own Bank. *It was a Community Bank and I realized that we owned the bank, but were being held hostages. The bad guys weren't mean, but controlling. Not scary, but in charge. Our money was in the bank. One person used their cell phone to call home to tell them to come get us out.*

Another person used a flashlight to try to send a signal out the window so we could be rescued. But it was light outside, so no one could see the flashlight. We knew that we would be killed eventually by the robbers. Someone said that we 'should all kneel on the floor in a circle and pray for God to deliver us'. But I say, 'No, that would be embarrassing. Besides they will kill us for sure then.'

I interpreted the dream then. Here are my words: Our unified vision is our investment in the Community Bank. The flashlight at the window was an attempt to get someone else to pull us along and rescue us when we face troubles/stalls with the vision. The captor is God. He has stalled the vision because of sin in our lives. He refuses to share His Glory with anyone and will bind us up if we proceed with the vision not His way. Cannot rely on the Program. Cannot rely on the students to need God.

There must be purity in the leaders and they must have God's vision above all else. Prayer is the key to unification of the Vision and Purity. Pride and unwillingness to sacrifice are impediments.

We need to pray for:
1. Humility
2. Willing heart of obedience
3. Sincere love for the brethren
4. Desire above all not to see souls go to Hell
5. That individuals assume responsibility for the purity of all the individuals on the team.
6. That individuals assume responsibility to have all people saved/ spirit fill and totally delivered.
7. Pray against apathy or passive attitude. Need a passion for the vision This is the first dream that I came truly to a verse that summed it up. Rev 12:10 Now has the salvation (Call To Me) and the Power (flashlight) and the authority (Our Bank) and the Kingdom of God (We are children of God). We are over comers because of the word of our testimony (get out of the building) and the Blood of the Lamb (Prayer). The two biggest hostage holders are spiritual pride and unwillingness to sacrifice self.

Learning How to Fight Satan Using the White rock

I began several weeks of focusing on Rev 12 and the war between God and Satan. God showed me that Satan's weapons are fear and fire. I kept thinking about a vision that I had earlier of a Serpent on the water coming for Pastor David. I reasoned that if Pastor David was in Las Vegas and the Serpent was in the Ocean, which made me on the beach. I started to get worried because it meant that I would face the

Serpent first. I asked God for help. He gave me a revelation as I hiked in the desert. He showed me a rock that was a different color in the inside. I memorized the verses Rev 3:11-12 and Jeremiah 23:29.

I was looking for the 'white rock'. D.J. Young prophesied over me again. He said, "There is a rock coming for you."

I asked him if it was a white rock, and He said, "No."

Then God showed me that first I have to break the rock that is coming for me to get to the white rock. It is inside the brown rock. Satan throws rocks at me and I have to break the rock by praying the Word of God.

When the rock is broken, then the black part will be made into flints to get the enemies and the white center will come to me. I asked God about the white rock with the new name. It's like a receiving the diamond on a wedding ring. It is symbolic of an intimate relationship.

The 'white rock' is revelation knowledge about Jesus Christ that comes to you as you pray through and break the stone.

Praying into God's Holiness to Part the Water

Then he showed me how to part the water and Go after the enemy. God showed me that if I pray into His Holiness, the water is parted to bring about His deliverance in our lives. My prayer for the Church was like the parting of the Red Sea. I walk on dry ground as I claim His Holiness for myself.

I put Him in front of me. His Word acts as lightening to part the water. When I claim the blood of Jesus over my sins, the water stacks up on both sides. If I sin, then the water starts to leak, like the tears of Jesus' over my sin. I will float and I will be face to face with the Serpent. But, if I stay in the crevice, the center of His Holiness covered under the purity of the Cross of Jesus, I am safe. Not only am I safe, Psalm 18 says that the lightening parts the water and the whole action causes a pursuit of the Serpent. The Serpent is then put on the run instead of lobbing you with stones. His action is crushed by God. Holy Prayer that is covered with the sanctification of the Blood of Jesus causes a spiritual collision between Satan and God.

The Holiness of God collides with the Serpent and destroys it. The heat from the lightening even tears up the rocks that are in the bed of the ocean and throws them down on other enemies. The rocks are made into flints.

Hearing God's Voice

I memorized Hebrews 1:1-4. God said that long ago He spoke through prophets, but now He has spoken through His Son. I rejected the gift of knowledge and went straight for the heart of God. I prayed through the entire book of Revelation after being prompted by a dream from one of my friends.

In the morning the Voice of God came to me audibly, "All these things will come to pass when the breath of the Lord blows against it."

I realized that what this meant was that; If God's Holy Spirit lives within me, then my breath becomes His Breath. The words of Scripture are just a book until they are activated through the Breath.

When they come out my mouth, God activates His Will. His Kingdom Comes.

Braiding the Father's Hair

My friend had a dream with me in it. She was leaving town and asked God if I would be 'OK'. In the dream I am braiding the Father's hair.

My interpretation: The strands are truths in the Bible and I take from one section and another section. He has shown me how to gather them and weave them to make central truths. My hands have been given to the Holy Spirit. The three strands are the Scriptures, Prayer, and the Holy Spirit.

On the Stairs to Heaven: Dream

Dream: Paul and I are on the stairs. It is like a set of stairs going up and across this field. There are different levels and different steps as you go along the way. The steps get kind of far away and steep right before the landing. I get scared and the sun 'blinds' me I cry out to him and he is right there to hold my hand and we walk together to the landing.

Then, I can see again. At the landing as we are holding hands, I ask, 'Shall we go up or down?"

He replies," We better go down and tell the rest of the people where the stairs are."

Interpretation: God has given me a helper on the stairs, but we are not unified. We both have relationships with God, but I am not depending on him for support. When I get into trouble, he will help and we will both have the same vision eventually; 'Salvation of souls'

Uncovering the Devil's Tactics

November I got into this study of how the Devil works. When I pray against him, It is like putting a mirror up to him. His deeds are all turned back on himself. He is in the merchandising business. His strength is in the 'beauty of his wisdom.'

When I pray the Scriptures, I hold up the true wisdom of God against Satan's own wisdom. The scriptures are a sword with a diamond tip. I became like 'Zorro' because I fight with a sword against the enemy's weapons. Because I have superior strength behind me and Holiness, then I will always be the hero of the people. Besides, my shadow looked like 'Zorro' with my hat on in the desert as I hike.

The battle will be fierce, and even on his back, Satan will declare, "I have won." Satan is like a pirate on the sea. He sees what he wants and because he knows that he is stronger and wiser than the other ship, he grabs the riches from the vessel. He relied on the anointing of God instead of the anointer. He stole God's honor and praise from men because he focused on the anointing and was 'awed' by it. He corrupted his wisdom because he was of magnificent splendor.

The wisdom became violent because he was looking through his own eyes and couldn't see much difference between God's beauty and his own. All he had to do was 'stop guarding the tree' and the woman's eyes were opened to see his viewpoint. He was judged by his own anointing as a guardian and protector.

He reminded himself of his violations. The fire from the midst of him consumed him. After he judged himself, God finished the process by turning him to ashes. He is like coal. It was burned instead of pressed in to diamonds. The raw material was changed in the finished product because they wasn't done yet. God stepped in and became a terror, and he became coal with ash instead of diamond. (Study of Ez 28)

Rock into the Pond: Vision

Nov 29, 2002 On an airplane, while I was praying for someone, I got a vision.

A very clear vision. It was a pebble being thrown into a pond. The pond is without waves at first and then the pebble is tossed into it. As it falls, it sends ripples through the water until the water reaches the boundaries. God showed me that prayer is like this. He is the rock, the

Word, and my prayer activates the movement of the rock. The Water is the Holy Spirit's action after the prayer has reached the ears of God. Prayer moves along the first ring (my primary intention), then on to another until it reaches the boundaries God has set for it. When God moves one person, they touch another, and so on developing a chain reaction within the Kingdom of God until His purposes have been met.

Revelation: Family Curses

God showed me about family curses when I asked on a prayer hike I asked God the question, "How does the past cause us problems now and how can we help the future?"

His answer: the past shadows the future. In a world that isn't round (with time) the shadow will never move and continue to shadow on and on. Satan works in the shadows. He can only shadow death as it has been conquered. He has shadowed with fear, pain and suffering.

God shines His light in to dispel the shadows. If you play in the dirt, you will find the valley of bones. You need to clean up your whole family line starting from Jesus---not Adam.

There was a vision: 'A spring starting in the desert.' Interpretation: The family is deceased, but God's spring is starting to give life to the promises that should have been dealt out and destroying curses. There is a slippery slide of sinful behavior in every family leading to captivity of the enemy. There is an hour glass; the sands of time VS the river of God. Sun in the eyes causes fear. Place an mirror in the eyes of the enemy to reflect himself and he will become scared. Hold up the glass- the diamond reflection of the diamond head sword becomes a full length mirror in the face of the enemy.

Ministry of Prayer as a Team

Dec 2002 I received prayer in a group setting. It is ministry prayer and we did as an exercise. The visions that the team seen were: A marshmallow, A flaming arrow on target, me above the road, some stairs up from the ocean to a lighthouse. Interpretations: the marshmallow is a symbol of softness and flexibility. The flaming arrow is being shot by the hand of God and means that I am on target in the things of God. The image of me above the road means I can see further down the road than normal (prophecy). The stairs leading up from the ocean is my heart for evangelism to rescue those that are drowning in the ocean. It is a vision of my heart to show many the way to safe land.

Getting to Know God's Character

On a prayer hike God showed me that as I could feel a hair on my arm tickling me, but not see it, I had to trust the spirit world was there. I needed to learn to 'feel' it rather than 'see' it.

First I must have faith to believe that what I feel is true, and then it will come. God sends the snow on all. He longs to give Himself to each of His children and a direct water supply. Nobody is to receive seconds when it comes to the true water of God.

He asked me to be a 'heart surgeon'. He will do the surgery, but He needs a pair of hands. He longs to do circumcision on hearts. What do I do with the sword? God told me that it is not a sword like a soldier carries, but a laser. He needs hands that will do 'exactly' what He wants them to do. He longs to get rid of the infestation of spirits.

They are like mosquitoes and tics that suck the blood out of people. They will continue to suck the blood of the heart of the person and chew until they chew through. When two tics meet, there is extreme inner turmoil as they fight it out for the same heart. The tics need to be burned off by God's laser. When you give your heart to God, Satan cannot use it for his lunch. After God burns off the tics, there are wounds that need to be healed from the inside.

Circumcision by God can be intimate and painful for people. Circumcision is an act of purification where we cut off the flesh in obedience to God. There is false circumcision: putting confidence in the flesh, or setting our minds on earthly things. (Phil 3). True circumcision is to place surpassing value in knowing Jesus, gain Him in my life, be found In Him, put on His righteousness and fellowship in His suffering, so we will be raised with Him.

The heart continues to be sick even though you have burned off the ticks. There needs to be a fleshly removal; a death to flesh and rebirth through faith in the working of God. He doesn't leave us diseased. He has already died to make us whole.

God only uses Diamonds on His Sword.

To gather the diamonds, you have to get them from the river. You will only find them when the light of God reflects on them in a certain way. (The diamonds are revelation knowledge about God that comes to us through prayer and testing.) You can't sift them out yourself because they are clear (pure). They can only been seen by their. As you stand in the river of the Holy Spirit, you will see the gem on the floor of the river, it takes faith as you grab it because as you bend down, there is a moment when you can't see it, but must believe that it is there.

When I go looking for the stone, I have to turn to the face of Jesus. That is when my heart gets engraved. I turn toward the laser beam. (II Corinthians 4:6). The new name is Revelation is circumcision of the heart by the master engraver. God's letter written on our hearts by the Holy Spirit, known and read by all men, being manifested that you are a letter of Christ.; Needle punch embroidery. God will make a heart stir to perform what He needs.

Prayer causes dreams in others; a whole church is changed. A friend came to me saying that there was a fight in her church because she wanted their church to pray as a team and the pastor was resistant. I prayed with her and the next week her pastor had a dream from God that told him that the foundation of his church was weak. He has started some prayer meetings.

Paul's Dream: Wall of Water

Jan 2003 Paul had a dream: *A wall of water was coming down from heaven and there were people all around in the desert. Some were on the lower ground and some were on the higher ground. He was on the higher ground. He saw the water was coming down fast and those on the lower ground were going to die. He said that he would be OK for a while, because he was on the higher ground.* No interpretation needed.

Revelation: Blocks, walls, locked doors

Walls. Sometimes people think that a door is locked, or they have a wall in front of them. Actually they are the ceiling, not the wall. You reach the wall when you go as far as your vision can take you. Then you need to cash it in for a new vision. The pillars hold up the Church. If a pillar is in one of the adjacent rooms, and needs to be moved, then it must be turned sideways and carried into the main sanctuary to be stood upright again.

You have to lay down your vision for the Church to be movable into the main sanctuary. (Rev 3:12) The Church pillars hold up the vision. If the pillar is too short, it is of no use to the building. The pillar is made of the core of the tree. Center cut and needs to be vertical to have the maximum strength and use. Maybe you think you are a cross member and God really wants to use you as a pillar. If you hang onto the things of the past and try to mix them with God's new vision it doesn't work.

You will feel like you have hit a wall. His vision will be the largest vision you can have. What are the needs for you that God sees? He looks from the top down. Tear the ceiling off your vision and allow God to impart to you and put His ceiling on it. If you reach a wall, what do you do? Look for the door first. If it is locked, then put yourself down (humble yourself and place your vision at His feet).

We have already been given the keys, so search yourself and your purse. What have you brought with you that is holding you back? If there is no door, then turn aside, not back. God longs to move us with His hands, not heavy equipment. The master builder has the plans for His Church and knows where the columns need to be placed. They are all based on the foundation in Him and revelation of His word to the individual.

Following the wrong vision will lead you to max out on your recourses and when they stop and your vision continues there will not be a closed door, but a wall without a door, a ceiling. How do you know?

Alignment with Him.

Revelation: The deeper the pain, the deeper the healing The pains inflicted on us through life's hurts are like the deep grooves in the mountainside. Deep sin and repentance also causes deep crevices. The snow falls deepest in these crevices and stays the longest. God's grace is deeper for those who have been forgiven much. I know, I have them.

I'm drowning: Dream

Jan 2003 Dream: *I am in our boat and Paul is in the boat with me. He wants me to stay in the boat, but I jump into the water. I tell him that I have to go. When I enter the water, my feet get stuck in the mud and the water comes up over my head. I am drowning. I yell at him, but he can't hear me because I am under the water. I can see the reflection of him leaning over the boat to see where I went.*

Interpretation: The urgency of God's call on my life causes me to forsake all and jump into the Holy Spirit (the water) even if it risks my relationship with Paul and my own life. The mire is my own sins and the problems that the enemy is throwing against me. I have taken on the responsibility to pray for everyone that I meet and it is overwhelming me to the point of drowning me. Not only am I drowning in the needs of others, I am stuck in my own sinful nature. I turned the ministry over to Him and rebuked Satan in my life. I believe I jumped from the boat because I was on fire for God.

Others Notice my Spirit of Prayer

Jan 2003 While I was at work, I was sitting at a makeshift desk in a patient's doorway and a friend came by to ask me to pray for her. As she left, I started to pray for her as I sat there in the chair.

When I went into the patient's room shortly, He asked me," Who were you praying for? I saw you kneeling in the doorway praying for someone?"

I never knelt, but his spiritual eyes were open and He saw my heart humbling myself before God. Amazing.

Uncovering the Spirit of Jezebel

Then I learn about Jezebel. She is a triad covered with fog.

1. Fear or inadequacy manifested in Control
2. Sorcery or witchcraft manifested in a white spirit
3. Deceit manifested in Rebellion (grumbling)

This is a separate writing. It was an intense process to uncover her. God gave me the story of 'Excalibur' to help unfold the mystery. I took the Scafford off. I uncloaked her and that left her defenseless. During the time there was intense warfare and I was actually approached by a spirit as I sat on the steps of the altar of the Church. I watched as an Angel protected me and the spirit reeled back when it tried to attack me.

Revelation: Raise the Level of Enlightenment

How do I raise the power of the Holy Spirit in my life? Enlighten. Raise the level of enlightenment. Raise the level of the boundaries that you have set for God in your mind. Don't limit yourself to the success God wants to give you.

Stop limiting God's blessing in your life.

Pray God will show me what the Keys to the Kingdom of God are used for. If you don't know what the key is to, then it will do you no good. The key has to have a door. I am to move among the Gems

Prayer Hike:

I hiked up a river bed to the top of a small peak. The rocks all became gems and the gems were Christians. They were many beautiful colors. There were some so large that they meshed right in with the rock of the peak. These are so close to God, you can't tell the difference. The river became a river of love flowing from the Rock washing over the gems. A mountain of flesh keeps us from the river.

It has to be conquered by faith in the Hand of God. I prayed for the gift of faith. Any sand in the river is washed down stream as the current picks it up. The larger jewels are closer to the top of the rock.

God spoke to me and said, "I will come in and out among the gems and find rest."

I am not to be stationary as one of the gems, but to do ministry with them. I weave amongst them and touch their lives as I go. I am on my way to the diamond at the top. I gathered rocks to give the ladies at the Women's Encounter.

The Key dream comes Alive

During a weekend Women's Encounter there was a feeling of disunity. Pastor called everyone together and had them stack their hands up like the members of a football team. He placed his hands on the top and bottom of the stack. Then he prayed for unity. Instantly, I saw the keys in my dream were like us. We were keys to the Kingdom of God. The bolt was the Holy Spirit unifying us.

The Alpha and Omega are on the top and bottom of us. We are centered in eternity to fulfill His wishes for His Kingdom Come.

Anointing

On Saturday night at the Encounter the Pastor came and spoke to us. He, then prayed over anyone who desired. The Holy Spirit was very powerful that night. Everyone he touched fell down. He would go back to people time after time each time they got up. We were thoroughly 'drunk' in the Spirit.

I remember rolling on the floor with a friend until She couldn't get up any longer. I went down three times, then Pastor came to me and he said, "Look at the mighty intercessor, She is just getting silly now."

I realized that he was right. I had came here looking for The Diamond that I had been praying into for a month. I wanted more of Jesus. More of Him. So, I got up and started praying to Him. I prayed so hard that I started to get chest pain. I surrendered myself totally to Him begging Him to give me MORE.

I continued to press-in to Him. Then I saw IT coming. I saw the Power of God hovering over me ready to touch down. It looked like the end of a huge drill bit. It was the most beautiful thing that I have ever seen. When it came down it didn't hit my head first, but the very center of my heart. It was beautiful light that swirled and swirled right through the center of my being. The color were flowing through me. They were turquoise, royal blue, and royal purple. Their .was a single gold thread woven through all of them.

Everything was alive and moving. I was lost in it; totally engulfed in the most wonderful feeling and beautiful priestly colors that I had ever know, or ever will know, I am sure. God is beautiful! It continued to swirl through my whole body and did not come out. The drill bore through my entire body and continued to encircle me with motion of light and feeling. Somehow the swirling colors picked me up and airlifted onto the rug.

When I regained consciousness, there was an overwhelming desire to Praise God. I couldn't get off of the floor for several hours. I just laid there and sang praises to God. They stepped over me as they packed up the room for the night. I didn't care, I was praising God from the floor. After probably 2 or 3 hours, I'm not sure, I went to my room. There, I continued to lay on the floor and praise God. After while, I moved to the bed.

But, I continued to praise God. I turned the music down as 2Am... then back on at 4Am starting in again. I believe God gave me the desire of my heart. He touched me.

The Pastor gave me a prophecy, "Don't kick down doors anymore. You don't need to. You have enough Bible in you and ability to lead a big Church in prayer."

Ladder: Vision

I saw a ladder in Church. Luke 18:10.

Religion VS relationship. People need to see a spirit that is willing to grow. Don't put yourself on a pedestal of pride. God gives grace to those who know they need God. We have to reverse the curse of sin in our lives (pride). We need a relationship with God built on trust, faith and belief in who He is. Relationship illuminates the love of God in your life. It brings revelation and illumination.

Reason VS revelation. God loves us and needs to be in control. He is asking for unification with us. If you want to have a relationship with God, then give him one. Ps 104

Crabs at my Grandmother's House: Dream

(Jan 28, 2003) I am at my Grandmother Rose's house near the beach. She lives on the beach in Washington State. My father and Stephanie Hope are on the doorstep. I am standing back a bit. My father knocks on the door and my grandmother opens the door from the inside. All of a sudden a multitude of sand crabs come running toward the door to get into the house.

They are walking sideways scampering toward the door. They crawled over the feet of the people in a rush for the door. There was a bid Red spider that came along with the crabs. It goes up Stephanie's leg. No one but me notices the crabs and the spider.

It was an infestation. I screamed at the spider. It was like a 'kiss of death' to Stephanie. I told the spider to leave her alone. When I did, it quickly crawled back down her leg and ran into the house with the other crabs.

Then I said to my father, "You know there are crabs going into the house."

He replied," It happens each season. We have to take care of them at the beach."

(It sounded like extermination done seasonally)

Initial interpretation: I realize that I was drilled out as a fiddler crab shell could be pealed off. All that is left is the central spiral. Iniquity (demons) fed on the trash in my life. The living trash, the flesh, draws them. The trash in my house calls to them. The trash has to be taken out regularly. The spider is Satan and he was rebuked from stealing my hope. When he couldn't steal my hope, he entered my house looking for stuff against me to kill my hope.

Secondary interpretation: This is the door to my house. On the porch is the Hope of my Salvation (Jesus) and my Father (God). My father knocks on the door. The hope is nearly destroyed by the spider, but is rebuked just in time. This door leads to the mysteries of my forefathers. A multitude of things rush on ahead of us through the door, my flesh, and sin. All of this infestation will be in the house when we enter. My father knows and expects it as part of the usual happenings for this season. It's the continual need for cleansing. I need cleansing from the curses of my forefathers, my own daily sin, and to rebuke the enemy.

Parallel Dream from a Friend Brings Salvation
(February 13, 2003) A friend at work met me at 0730 AM and said that she had 'the weirdest dream last night. She dreamed that her and I were at a bar eating crabs. The bar had a one way door. You could go in, but not out. There was beer but we weren't drinking it. We just kept on eating these King crabs.'

The interpretation: The crabs are sin. We are feasting at the table of Jesus presence because we have entered the door. Our sin has been taken away and our life has been turned into dining experience. We dine on our enemies. The one way door indicates that it is a once and for all decision. Christ paid the price once and for all for our sins. My first dream speaks of my need to ask daily forgiveness for sins and

to rebuke the Devil. The second dream speaks of the once and for all forgiveness that Jesus offers by his sacrifice for us. I asked her to come over to my house and I interpreted the dream for her using my dream. Then I led her to Christ at the kitchen table.

Revelation: Kicking down Doors
I realized that I am not kicking down the doors, but kicking against going through the door that God has for me. He longs to give me gifts, like keys, to open the doors. I Sam 2:28 Did I not chose you to by my priest, to go up to my altar, to burn incense, to carry ma ephod before me: and did I not give to the house of your father all the fire offerings of the sons of Israel?

Why do you kick at my sacrifice and at my offering which I have commanded in my dwelling by making yourselves fat with the choicest of every offering of my people?

When I asked God how I ended up here, he said that it was because of my great-grandmother Grace. By Grace I was saved, through her faith, not of myself...it is a gift of God. He selected me and as he has sacrificed His son, and His son has paid the price for Him to do his work in my life, I am being rebellious by refusing to go the way he wants me to go. I have refused assignment as Eli's sons refused assignment. He has shown me things in the spirit and I have refused to believe they were true and have not prayed into them for the people of the Church. I have doubted that the spiritual visions were from him. I have become fearful thinking I was making stuff up or being tricked by the enemy. I have wanted to keep control and use my own sword. I covered it with a cloak of spirituality.

I felt inferior and that I could not be used by him. This triad is Jezebel. If God has given you a key and you believe it is the right key, then you will be persistent to jiggle the key until it goes into the slot to open the door. Faith is the answer. Without the spirit of Jezebel and with the spirit of faith: I Samuel 2:35 "But I will raise up for myself a faithful priest who will do according to what is in my heart and in my soul: and I will build him an enduring house, and he will walk before my anointed always."

Driving me as a Peg

God wants me to drive a tent peg. The peg goes through the flesh to the cross of Jesus Christ. It is his bittersweet plan to heal our suffering by his suffering. This is the only way He can offer us all the blessings of His marvelous Kingdom. Ezra 9:8 But now for a brief moment grace has been shown from the Lord our God, to leave us an escaped remnant and to give us a peg in his holy place that our God may enlighten our eyes and grant us a little reviving in our bondage. I Samuel 2:35 God Himself will raise up- He will train me himself.

I John 2:27 As for you the anointing which you received from Him abides in you and you have no need for anyone to teach you; but as His anointing teaches you about all things, and is true and is not a lie, and just as it has taught you, abide in him. He jealously desires His Spirit that he has made to dwell in us.

He longs to make me into a covenant of peace like Phinehas. Numbers 25:10. The peg that goes through Jesus flesh has to be driven by us.

That nail becomes the peg that the church hangs on the tent peg.

Anointed in front of the Church

Pastor David anointed me with Oil in front of the Church for an Intercessor of Prayer. I wanted it so bad last year, but it wasn't for me then. Now, I just know that it is true. God didn't have me walk into the anointing, but rather grow to a point that He could anoint me. I feel that I have reached a new level with the dreams. I know that they have scriptural meaning. Also, after the Encounter, I have a new transparency with other people. I open myself up to others and this allows God to connect with them on an intimate level.

The say,' this has to be God because no one could have known this about me.' It's about learning to know the soul of God.

Sea City Dream

Paul and I are given a city to manage. It is along the coast, like in California. It looks expensive. There are a lot of large trees and grassy areas. No central business area. I am eager to introduce him to two people. One guy who will give him the power (land management). He owns the land and has the policies. The other guy who will give him the authority; he is like the sheriff. Both are kind of smucky and want stuff in exchange for favors. Paul is not interested in meeting them and gets sidetracked looking at this old jail in the middle of the town. It is one of those jails that holds just one prisoner. It looks pretty secure, but is empty now.

A Burning Bush

We are a bush that burns.
But, is not consumed
but, only for those around us
to witness the awesome power of God.

Then, I heard a loud voice in heaven say: Now have come the salvation and the power and the kingdom of our God, and the authority of his Christ. For the accuser of our brothers, who accuses them before our God day and night, has been hurled down. They overcame him by the blood of the Lamb and by the word of their testimony: they did not love their lives so much as to shrink from death. Revelation 12.10.

Addendum:

As I release this writing, I know that by my testimony many will see what God is able to do with someone who is willing to seek Him, not being worried about what it costs to get there.

You can read the story of the building of the business: Glorybound Publishing in the book ***Dove Dreams Fly***. Believe me, it has been worth it. All of the psychotic sleepless nights have been worth it to hear His voice. It's the voice of God.

My prayer for you is that you will be inspired to ask Him to open up the avenues for you to hear Him as I have.

Scooped up by the Father

He is calling, we just need to learn how to get on His channel to be able to hear the words.

I called out to Him and He answered I cried with all my strength and He came like a Father running to a fallen child, He scooped me up, and cradled me in His arms. And, I never left.

New Goulashes

Enveloped in your love. I will ever be. Surrounded by
Your goodness, your faithfulness, your everlasting kindness.
For, I had tripped like a child with new goulashes on. I was face
down in the mud and You lifted me up. And, I had lost one of my
shoes in the puddle. You retrieved it. You didn't say anything
about them. My momma had given them to me. She got them
second hand. They didn't fit, but I wore them anyway.
It was all I had. But, like a tender father, You didn't
say anything until I noticed. You just took my hand
and lifted me from the place where I was covered
with mud and wiped me with the handkerchief
that was is your own pocket. You didn't
say anything about how clumsy I was. I
thought it, but I never said it either. But,
then, You lifted me up into Your arms.
Then, it happened. My shoes fell
off. I didn't notice
because
I didn't need
them anymore.
I was being carried
by my Father.
Still, we
didn't say anything. We didn't need to. We were
face to face, heart to heart, cheek to cheek my eyes
to yours. The window to our Souls had been opened.

KAPASEUS INDEX

A Burning Bush	142		Hail to the King	105
A Matter of Weaving	75		Hands of Grace	48
A Memorial Day	13		Held in His Affection	102
A Model in the Way	32		Help on the Other Side	79
Anointing Sprinkles	77		His Pearl	11
Adoration Lift	114		Hold the Vine	24
Be Threaded	8		Honoring Grand Father	85
Being Stirred	45		Imprinted Plans	48
Beneficial to God	26		In Love	114
Boxed Options	83		Joining Spirits	112
Brought on Through	92		Keel of Direction	561
Canopy	74		Keyhole	25
Cap-Sized Ship	70		Left Handed Christians	93
Choosing our own Vehicles	44		Levels of Preparedness	38
Colorful Threads of God	84		Life Dreams and Visions	21
Coming over the Ridge	80		Lighting the Candle	41
Coordinated Flow	77		Lot's Wife	94
Crafts	26		Manifestation of Glory	35
Crystal Clear Communion	55		My God Grew Yesterday	87
Draw Bridge of Faith	52		My Testimony	116
Emancipation Declaration	25		Miracle Anointing	22
Envision the Revision	60		New Goulashes	145
Fabric of Say	78		New in You	37
Faith as a Mustard Seed	62		Owning Kingdoms	63
Ferrying Gifts	23		Palms of Love	91
Fluffy Prayer	58		Pass the Shuttle	66
Fly to His Aspirations	72		Pitiful Faith	68
Four Dream Tapestry	97		Pop Beads	77
Gift Extension	79		Power Reach	64
Given Too Much	50		Pray in Flags	41
Glory Pass	14		Press	47
God of Comfort	82		Print and Imprint	47
God's Oreo	28		Prophecy Threads	57
Green Light at Work	36		Pure Vessel	108

Pushed by a Hand	59
Railroaded Gifts	57
Rock Through the Window	103
Rope	40
Running Along the Trail	43
Seam Ripper	81
Spool of Your Heart	53
Team Leaders	101
Telepathic Fishing	115
Temptation Obstructs Justice	57
Tangled Threads of Hope	68
The Cabinet of Your Heart	60
The First is Last	100
Threaded Through His Purity	36
Threaded Through Training	51
Threads of God's Voice	20
Threads of Hope	64
Threads of Praise	20
Threads of Mercy	96
Too Much	49
Tools on our Knees	31
Twirled and Wrapped	56
Twisted too Tight	54
Unobstructed Breathing	27
Walking on my Hands	86
Weaving the Picture	67
Will you Still Love Me, Then?	29
Wisdom	15

About the Author

Sheri Hauser grew up in Seattle, Washington accustomed to the rainy days and nights going on long hikes in the Cascades in the summer and snow skiing in the winter. She graduated from High School in Leavenworth, Washington and attended Bible College in Oregon. Married at 20, she went on to nursing school and had two children. In 2001, she began writing spiritual books and started to look for a publisher. Not finding one who would accept her manuscript, she opted to learn what was needed to grow her own publishing company. Initially the company was called Glory Bound Books and obtained license in Las Vegas in 2005. As the company grew, she tossed her entire nursing paycheck into purchasing printers and software. She attended classes at the University of Las Vegas for graphic design, web site development and photo shop. It took three years of intensive study to learn papers, the publishing industry and how to put books together. Throughout this time, she developed the Lasertrain (a set of digital templates for making your own books). She climbed the ladder of her profession and after 30 years as a Cardiothoracic Nurse in Intensive Care, she retired from nursing full-time to dedicate her time to grow a publishing company. By 2016, she had written 25 books, and published over 600 books (from authors).

Her and her husband relocated to Camp Verde, Arizona in 2017 and set the publishing company in an old house living in the upstairs. They love the quiet cowboy town and she is presently active in forming a newly developing Chamber of Commerce. She is the president. Additionally, she is part of the Curriculum Development Team and a Facilitator teaching classes related to publishing at Osher Life Long

Learning Institute in Sedona, Clarkdale and Camp Verde.
2020 started off with a bang when she began doing ads on Amazon for her books. Today, she has 15 books on page 1 of their topic search engines and is actively seeing sales daily.

Sheri Hauser is the author of several series of books including: Glorybound Lasertrain, Dream Books with Steps to Intimacy with God, GBK Children's books and a couple of text books on publishing.

Glorybound Publishing

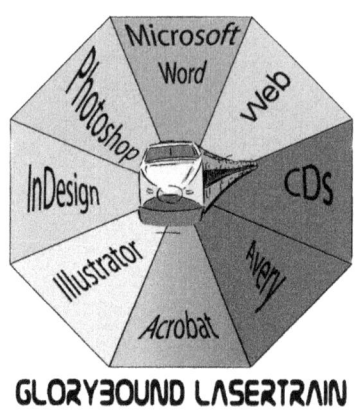

Sheri's Books

The manuals are books which help prepare for the release of the prophetic wave of the Holy Spirit as spoken of in Joel 2. These books are written from dreams. The dreams were given over a period of around 6 months or so. As they were received, I carefully interpreted them using Scriptures. Then I was given an outline dream. The dreams of the specific subject were then put into the outline. That forms the books. There are 21 books. Initially, all of the books were as one giant book. Then as I received more dreams of direction, the books began to split; first into four, then into more (like bread rising in a bowl) they grew over time within the right environment. The first book split into what became the first four books. I was instructed to turn over the stack and release them. So, I released Coriantá, having it professionally edited and printed at the cost of $37,000. By the time I got to the next book, I realized that the books were reproducing at an alarming rate, and I would never have enough money to print them conventionally, so I asked God if I could have a publishing company.

He said, "Sure."

I quickly responded, "I don't know anything about a publishing company."

His response, "That's OK. It will come in a box with instructions."

I quickly called the guy who put together my first book and then ordered the computer program which he specified as the one for making books. Guess what? It came in a box with instructions. (Smile). Several of the books sprouted due to the response from individuals asking questions--such as *Simple Fun Christian Dream Interpretation*, the three books in the Prophetic Prayer Series as well as *Prophetic Interpretation of Art*.

All of the books are available as e-books and bound copies regular and large print through Amazon.com. Printed bound, signed, color editions are available directly through Glorybound Publishing. Use the contact page on the web site to order.

The Prophetic Wave

Manuals for a Prophetic Wave of the Holy Spirit with Miracles, Signs and Wonders

And Afterwards I will Pour Out My Spirit
Dream Language Understood
Faith on a Wing and a Prayer
Filled with the Holy Spirit
Going to the Center of God's Heart
Growing Ministry to Seed instead of Fruit
Intimate Relationship with Jesus
Living in the Haunted House of my Head
Living in the Shadow of the Sins of our Parents
Preparing the Bride of Christ: Allegorical
Sharing Prophetic Gifts in the Church
Simple Fun Christian Dream Interpretation
Spiritual Authority Over Demon Dragons
Tactical Demonic Warfare
Why the Glory Departed

Prophetic Prayer
Foundational Prophetic Prayer
Leading Prophetic Prayer
Manual of Personal Prophetic Prayer

Prophetic Arts
Christian Authors Driving the Market
Inspirational 3-D Poetry
Prophetic Interpretation of Art

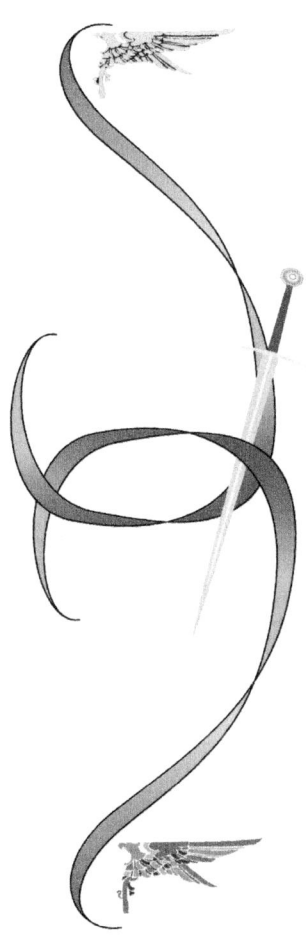

Made in the USA
Middletown, DE
28 December 2020